James Boswell

(1740 –1795)

THE SCOTTISH PERSPECTIVE

The Younger Boswell: while on the Grand Tour, in Rome, *1765*
by George Willison.

James Boswell
(1740–1795)

THE SCOTTISH PERSPECTIVE

Roger Craik

The Faculty of Advocates

EDINBURGH:HMSO

British Library Cataloguing in Publication Data.
A catalogue record for this book is available from the British Library.

ISBN: 0 11 494226 9

Contents

Acknowledgements

THE STARTING POINT for a book such as this, must be the vast scholarly output of Boswell material sponsored by the Editorial Committee of the Yale Editions of the Boswell papers. Details of the various Boswell journals published over the years are given in the Bibliography. I have drawn freely on these and on the definitive scholarly biographies by Frederick Pottle and Frank Brady, covering Boswell's earlier and later years respectively.

In about 1986, through the auspices of the Auchinleck Boswell Society, I had the great good fortune to meet Dr Irma Lustig, a member of the Editorial Committee and co-editor of two of the journals. Dr Lustig was kindness itself to me, helped me complete my collection of Boswell materials and arranged a meeting for me with members of the committee at Yale. Most important, however, she encouraged me to feel that there was scope for a biography of Boswell, written from the Scottish viewpoint and that I might be able to write it. I hope that the finished book justifies her encouragement.

Various people and institutions have helped in various ways. Dr Thomas Crawford and Dr John Strawhorn revised various parts of the manuscript. I found Dr Strawhorn's comments and suggestions in relation to his home county of Ayrshire, particularly helpful. I would also like to thank Ian Gow of the Ancient Monuments Commission for valuable background material on the history of Auchinleck House and James Simpson of Messrs. Simpson and Brown, Architects, for his kind permission to reproduce the floor and elevation plans of the house. The Historic Buildings Trust (the present owners of Auchinleck House) generously gave permission for the reproduction of photographs of the building. Dr Athol Murray, former Keeper of the Records for Scotland, was the source of the entry relating to Boswells marriage in the Stewarton parish register. Dr Iain G Brown, and the staff at the National Library of Scotland, generously supplied photographs of Boswell's Consultation Book and manuscript Library Catalogue. Raymond Docherty, clerk to the Faculty of Advocates (the sponsors of this book) took time to answer various queries on obscure aspects of 18th century Faculty practice. G T Herd and Ian Spence of Toronto supplied me with interesting background material on Mrs Dodds and Archibald Douglas respectively (see Chapter 6).

My colleague Sheriff Martin Mitchell, who helped to mount the 1973 National Library of Scotland exhibition commemorating the 200th anniversary of the Highland Jaunt, supplied copies of certain of the photographs then used. Mrs M Finlay, my long serving secretary, bravely battled with the manuscript and the staff at HMSO (particularly Alastair Holmes and Gillian Kerr) proved extremely helpful in the various stages of the book's production.

Finally, I would like to say a special thank you to my wife, Helen. She has had to live, albeit vicariously, with James Boswell for more years than I dare say she cares to remember. In matters Boswellian, her patience and forbearance must approach those of Mrs Margaret Boswell herself. As a small quid pro quo, I dedicate this book to her.

Edinburgh
October 1994.

PUBLISHERS ACKNOWLEDGEMENTS

The publishers are grateful to the following for their permission to reproduce photographs:

The Scottish National Gallery, the Scottish National Portrait Gallery, the National Portrait Gallery, London, the Trustees of the National Library of Scotland, the Trustees of the British Museum, the Victoria and Albert Museum, Edinburgh City Libraries, The Ayrshire Tourist Board, Dumfries and Galloway Tourist Board, Joe Rock, Photographer, Messrs Simpson and Brown, Sheriff Martin Mitchell, The Faculty of Advocates and the author, Roger Craik.

Every effort has been made to obtain permission to reproduce and acknowledge the illustrations used in the book, but if anyone has inadvertently been overlooked, the Publishers will be pleased to make appropriate arrangements at the earliest suitable opportunity.

Particular thanks are also due to Vivian Bone at Edinburgh University Press for her help in securing permission to reproduce extracts from the Boswell papers. All material is printed with permission of Yale University and Edinburgh University Press.

Preface

James Boswell is a neglected literary figure in his native Scotland. Ask any Scottish child over eight years old what he or she knows of Robert Burns and you will have a positive reaction. Even a mention of Sir Walter Scott (long the hero of the Scottish literary establishment) will provoke a reaction of sorts from the older Scots child. Robert Louis Stevenson is still held in great affection by the more literary Scot, though some would be surprised to learn that he was himself a Scotsman. But a mention of James Boswell will draw a nigh universal blank, even in his home county of Ayrshire.

The situation is largely Boswell's own fault. Part of him would be an Englishman. His most private writings are laced with the desire to cut a figure in London and display a loathing of the more homespun aspects of Scottishness. The considerable status which he eventually did achieve was in a London literary context: the great biographer of a great Englishman. Throughout his life Boswell strove to iron out his Scottishness. 'I do indeed come from Scotland, but I cannot help it,' were his very first words to Dr Johnson.

But part of Boswell was very Scottish and remained so. His opening self-introductory words to Jean-Jacques Rousseau were: 'I am a Scots gentleman of ancient family' (letter, 3 December 1764). He was immensely proud of his Scottish family background and of the family estate of Auchinleck. He was born in Scotland and his formative years were passed there. He was a Scots lawyer by training, and the bulk of his professional life was spent in Scotland. He lies buried in the family vault in Auchinleck.

On this, the eve of the bi-centenary of the author's death, it is time for Boswell to be seen in a Scottish context. The last study of Boswell, as a Scot, was in 1896 and even that was written to 'materially add to the correct understanding and the enjoyment of Boswell's great work: *The Life of Johnson*' (W.K. Leask, Famous Scots Series, *James Boswell*). Since then there have been great strides in Boswellian scholarship. The rest of the world has taken up James Boswell, even if Scotland has been slow to do so.

This book reviews Boswell's life and work from a Scottish point of view. It would be unrealistic to ignore completely his achievements in England and Europe, but the purpose of this work is to place the emphasis on the background from which the achievements sprang.

The school child in Auchinleck's Main Street may yet hear more of James Boswell.

CHAPTER 1

Antecedents

James Boswell was born in his father's house in Blair's Land, Parliament Close, Edinburgh, on 29 October 1740. His father, Alexander Boswell, was a leading Scottish advocate and heir to the family estate in Auchinleck, Ayrshire. Boswell was the eldest son of his father's marriage to Euphemia Erskine, 'a gentle, pious, mystical lady, of an aristocratic Scots family', as he described her to Rousseau. The Boswells themselves, although lairds, rather than lords, had been established at Auchinleck since the early part of the sixteenth century.

These bare facts at once tell us much about the kind of person that James Boswell was. First, he was a Scotsman and, though he would sometimes deny it in later life, he was basically proud of being Scottish. But in the latter half of the eighteenth century there was a strong-running tide of Anglophilia. Tutors were engaged to purge 'Scotticisms' from the English of the Scots gentry. It was becoming unfashionable to speak broad Scots. On many occasions in later life, Boswell was to cringe at overt displays of Scots manners. But, even as late as 1791, Boswell was to affirm his basic Scottishness in a piece of autobiographical writing which appeared in the *European Magazine* for May and June of that year. He opens his description of himself by telling the reader that he was 'the eldest son of Alexander Boswell, Esq., an eminent Judge in the Supreme Courts of Session and Justiciary in Scotland, by the title of Lord Auchinleck, from the Barony of that name in Ayrshire, which has been the property of the family for almost three centuries...'

Second, although the family roots and family seat were in Ayrshire, the

Auchinleck House, c.1760, built by Boswell's father.

family professional fortunes were in Edinburgh. Boswell's own career was to be at the Scottish Bar. Once his travels in Europe were complete (1763-66), he was largely to divide his time between Edinburgh, London and Ayrshire. It has been said (by Professor F.A. Pottle the leading expert on Boswell) that he 'remained at heart a town man all his life'. It is difficult to dispute this, although, latterly at least, it is clear that he had a good working knowledge of his estate and its management. But Edinburgh was to be the stage upon which the young Boswell would take his first literary and professional bows. The city was also to be his main home until he became Laird of Auchinleck in 1782 and finally moved to London in 1786. For the bulk of his life, then, Boswell was an Edinburgh man. But the family background was in Ayrshire.

At the time of James Boswell's birth, the Boswell family had been established at Auchinleck for almost two and a half centuries. The Auchinleck family was itself a branch of the even more venerable Boswell family of Balmuto in Fife. The successive lairds had been soldiers, farmers and, latterly, professional men. Boswell's father and grandfather had both been successful advocates. The practice of advocate in eighteenth-century Scotland, was geared to suit the requirements of its predominantly land-owning practitioners. The court terms were such as to allow the lawyer/land-owners to attend to their estates in the crucial seasons of

The old Kirk and Boswell family mausoleum, Auckinleck.

springtime and autumn. Even yet, the Scottish court 'vacations' reflect this pattern, although, for the busy practitioner, these have long ceased to be times when court work could be suspended.

A good portion of every year, then, was spent on the family estate. Auchinleck lies in pleasant, green countryside, within sight of the Lanarkshire hills to the east. It is situated in the heart of Ayrshire, some twelve miles east of Ayr. Auchinleck estate lies to the west of the village of the same name. That village was created by James Boswell's father in 1756 and grew into a sizeable town in the nineteenth century as coal mining was developed in the area. But now the mines have closed, the town has a depressed air, and the main street is sadly decrepit. Off that main street is the Barony Church, built in 1837, and beside it the old parish church which it superseded, and in which the Boswells worshiped. Within the last twenty-five years the old church has been restored and reroofed by local enthusiasts of the Auchinleck Boswell Society. The building now houses the museum of the society. It also has, as an annexe, the crypt which serves as the Boswell family mausoleum. On the outside wall is the family emblem of the hooded hawk and the family motto: 'Vraye Foy', and within lie the remains of James Boswell and his family.

The estate itself lies a mile or two to the west. The heart of the estate lies between the steep gullies formed by the Lugar Water and the tributary Dipple Burn. Where these two streams converge, about a mile before the confluence joins the River Ayr, is a rocky, wooded eminence. Here stood the first stronghold of the Auchinleck Boswells. Today there remain only a few mounds of stone in the undergrowth. The scene, however, is dramatic. The riverbank falls away steeply to the waters of the burn below, and in the near distance opposite are the ruins of the ancient Castle of Ochiltree. As early as the visit of Francis Grose, the antiquary, in 1789, the old castle had been but a picturesque fragment. An engraving of the ruins appears in volume 2 of Grose's *Antiquities of Scotland.*

In the early seventeenth century a more convenient family residence had been built a short distance away. This, too, was abandoned by the family when the present house was constructed in the early 1760s. More substantial ruins of the second house remain, with vaulted cellars and walls still rising to a height of fifteen feet or so. Constructed in red sandstone, the house must have been a pleasant and secure laird's home. It is said to have had lovely gardens, maintained until quite recently. James Boswell as a child came to stay in this old house in his grandfather's time, and more frequently when his father succeeded to the estate in 1749.

But by the time of Grose's visit the second house is said to have been unroofed. As he puts it in his *Antiquities:* 'These at present belong to James Boswell, Esquire, well known to the public by diverse ingenious publications. He resides in a handsome, modern seat adjoining.'

The handsome, modern seat was constructed by Boswell's father, who had become Lord Auchinleck in 1754. It remains a most imposing building. The house itself is constructed in the solid mid-eighteenth-century style, made popular and well known by the Adam family. The architect of the mansion is not known. The grey stone façade of the house is broken up by four tall vertical pillars, rising the height of the house and appearing to support a massive triangular pediment. This is decorated by an astonishing profusion of carved stonework. There are depicted, in flamboyant fashion, all the trappings of a judge's office. The hooded hawk surmounts all. As the Duchess of Northumberland reported in her diary after a visit in 1760: 'Went to Auchinlech [sic] the seat of Mr Boswell, Lord Auchinlech, who has just built a new house, the Pediment is terribly loaded with Ornaments of Trumpets and Maces and the Deuce knows what. It is but a middling house, but justly, it is a romantick spot.' At eaves level, the walls are surmounted by a massive balustrade with five classical urns flanking and crowning the pediment. This was indeed a handsome seat for a Lord of Session and his impressionable son.

The ornate pediment and east elevation of Auchinleck House.

At the bottom of the pediment, Lord Auchinleck has had inscribed a motto: 'Quod petis hic est, Est Ulubris, animus si te non deficit aequus'. Auchinleck was to be the country retreat where the scholar and man of business could be at rest if he had sufficient strength of mind. Given the mercurial disposition of his son, this motto on the family home is ironic to say the least. It might almost have been selected by the father to remind James of his responsibilities.

The house is flanked by two curving wings which terminate in elaborate stone gazebos. The wings are of a different stone and were added in the 1770's. In the writer's opinion, they detract from the appearance of the house, but this is doubtless a question of taste.

Internally, the house is surprisingly compact. There is a good-sized dining room on the ground floor with an impressive plaster ceiling remaining. There is a large drawing room. On the upper floor, encompassing four bays of windows, and looking out over the open country to the west, is the old library, now an empty shell, but in Boswell's day, full of literary treasures. In his account of the *Tour to the Hebrides* with Dr Johnson, Boswell records (2 November, 1772) that: 'my father showed Dr Johnson his library, which, in curious editions of the Greek and

Roman classicks, is, I suppose, not excelled by any private collection in Great Britain.'

Boswell's direct descendants ceased to live in Auchinleck House at the beginning of the present century. The library and contents were sold off in various lots in 1893, 1906 and 1917 as was the bulk of the estate a few years later. The mansion was, however, bought in 1920 by Colonel John Boswell, a descendant of another branch of the family, and it remained in Boswell occupation until the middle 1960s, when deterioration of the fabric necessitated a move to a cottage on the estate. A remaining part of the estate is still in Boswell hands. The present laird, James Boswell, is enthusiastic and accommodating to those who show a genuine interest.

The more recent history of the house is encouraging. After a period of neglect, vandalism and decay, it was handed over in 1988 to the Scottish Historic Buildings Trust. Under its auspices, the fabric has been rendered wind - and watertight, although the question of future use of the house presently remains an open one.

Auchinleck, of course, has to be viewed against the backdrop of Ayrshire, that attractive county of rolling hills and green fields, falling to the sea.

The area remains predominantly rural. This is particularly so since the intervening veneer of industrialisation (particularly coal mining) has recently diminished. In Boswell's day, it was a county of large estates, small-holdings and tenant farms. On the extended Auchinleck estate alone there were 104 farms, several of them extensive hill farms, but mostly small holdings of less than 100 acres. Altogether Auchinleck estate covered more than 20,000 acres, and around 800 men, women and children dwelt on the estate, including those in the village, all dependent upon the Boswells. But the prevalent hardship, the wretched housing and primitive communications of the eighteenth century should also be kept in mind. Infant and adult mortality was high, poverty and disease endemic. The typical Ayrshire character is, however, robust and resilient, allowing life to proceed cheerfully enough for the most part. Religious opinions were strongly held and religious observances firmly enforced. The Covenanting tradition was strong in the south-west of Scotland. However, religious prejudices did not constrict Boswell, who flirted briefly with Catholicism as a young man, cheerfully attended Anglican services in London, and was a regular member of the congregation of Auchinleck Kirk, latterly as laird and patron.

At the heart of the area, attractively situated on an extensive bay, lies the county town of Ayr. The spectacular peaks of the Isle of Arran lie across the Firth of Clyde to the north-west. To the south, the strand of Ayr Bay runs on to a headland crowned by the ruins of Greenan Castle. It is a town much loved by its inhabitants: 'Auld Ayr which ne'er a town surpasses, for honest men and bonnie lassies', as Burns put it in his tale of 'Tam O'Shanter' (1791). In Boswell's day, the town was still small and had fewer than 4,000 inhabitants. The original old town extended, for the most part, along the High Street and Sandgate to the south of the river. The river was (and still is) spanned by the Auld Brig, an ancient, hump-backed structure, although a later and more elegant bridge now carries the town traffic across to the northern suburbs.

Boswell had often to repair to the county town on estate, legal and political business. He had a wide circle of friends among the neighbouring gentry and a business visit was often tempered by conviviality.

Today, it has to be said, little remains of the atmosphere of old Ayr. Certainly the Auld Kirk (1656) stands, happily intact, in its surrounding graveyard. Substantial portions of the walls of the Cromwellian Fort can also be seen here and there among the modern houses. But, for the most part, successive generations of burgh councillors have replaced historic buildings to facilitate passage and trade. A walk along the bustling main streets of Ayr is not an evocative experience. Only in the area around the Auld Brig is it still possible to feel something of the couthy atmosphere of the Ayr of Burns and Boswell.

But to return to Auchinleck and the Boswell family. Both James Boswell's father and grandfather were lawyers. Both were members of the Scottish Bar, as James was to be himself. The grandfather, also James, was admitted as a member of the Faculty of Advocates in 1698. He is said to have had a large practice but appears to have been a bit of a plodder: so slow, indeed, that he is said never to have understood a cause until he lost it three times. In his invaluable reminiscences of the time, Ramsay of Ochtertyre describes the grandfather as 'a slow, dull man of unwearied perseverance and unmeasurable length in his speeches'. Be that as it may, at the time of his death in 1749, when James the younger was nine, he left the estate in financial good heart so as to enable both his son Alexander and his grandson to improve and profit by it.

Alexander Boswell (1707-82) was to become a Lord of Session, as Lord Auchinleck, in 1754. He was a dominant figure in his son's life. One of the most prominent Scottish lawyers of his day, he played a large part in the affairs of the Faculty of Advocates and in public life. Ramsay obviously

Alexander Boswell (1707 - 82):
Boswell's father
and stern mentor.

considered him a much more weighty figure than his son. In Ramsay's published reminiscences, Lord Auchinleck merits some twelve pages, while young James (described as an 'untoward genius') only receives attention as a living thorn in the venerable father's flesh.

Lord Auchinleck was a great classical scholar. One of the treasures of Auchinleck, now at Yale, is a manuscript catalogue of the Auchinleck library taken by James's wife, Margaret, shortly after Boswell's accession to the estate in 1782. The catalogue records page after page of Greek and Latin classics collected by Margaret's father-in-law. In the fashion of the times, Lord Auchinleck studied civil law at Leyden and was called to the Bar in December 1729. According to Ramsay, at the time of the Rebellion in 1745, Alexander was 'a lawyer much esteemed but not in great practice'. Although Lord Auchinleck's reputation has come down to us over the centuries with a certain grimness about it, he does appear to have had his lighter side. He is said to have been seen 'strutting abroad in red heeled shoes and red stockings while a student in Paris'.

In 1748 Alexander was appointed as the first Sheriff-Depute of Wigtownshire (heritable jurisdictions having been abolished in 1747 following the '45 Rebellion). He played a prominent part in the affairs of the Faculty as one of their examiners of entrants and as a curator of the

Euphemia Erskine (1718 - 76):
Boswell's gentle, pious, mother.

Advocates Library. He was also elected as one of the Faculty
Representatives to promote the 1752 Proposals of the Convention of Royal
Burghs for the improvement of Edinburgh (of which more anon).

That James the younger was in some awe of his father can hardly be
doubted. The first preserved early journal of Boswell *(Journal of the
Northern Circuit, May 1761)* records his impressions of a trip to Inverness
with his father as the circuit judge. The young Boswell records that it was
pleasing to see his father so easy with the servants of the Court and the
local dignitaries. In truth, the father seems to have been typical of a type of
Scots professional man, still frequently to be met in the city clubs: easy and
affable with his social equals in an informal setting; haughty and distant,
both at business and away, to his juniors and social inferiors.

It must be said that there appears to have been little in the make-up of
either father or grandfather to have spawned the mercurial disposition of
James Boswell. As to his mother, little is known. She was of noble family,
an Erskine of Mar, and there were royal connections in her ancestry. The
snob in Boswell was extremely proud of this fact. He described himself to
Rousseau as 'a Scots gentleman of ancient family'. In a sketch of his early
life, also written by him for the elucidation of the great philosopher, he
described his mother as being 'extremely kind' and 'too anxious' for his

well-being. She was also 'extremely pious'. It is clear that Boswell was very fond of his mother. He described himself as being 'stunned' and 'stupefied' at the news of her death in 1766, when he heard of it in Paris, as he was travelling homewards on the last leg of his Grand Tour. Perhaps the contrast between the strict, sober, intellectual father and the gentle, over-indulgent mother helps to explain the extraordinarily volatile nature of Boswell's own character. By contrast with his father, Boswell seemed absurd, eccentric and mischievous to Ramsay and to many other of his more sober contemporaries. How many other sons of strict upbringing have rebelled against it when given their heads?

Boswell was the eldest of three surviving children, all boys. His brother John was three years younger, and David eight. John was to become a soldier and was latterly mentally deranged. David was to be a merchant, long resident in Spain. Boswell's early years were divided between stays at Auchinleck and in Edinburgh. Much of his education took place at home. His first tutor was John Dun, later to become minister at Auchinleck. Boswell described him to Rousseau as

> *not without sentiment and sensibility. He began to form my mind in a manner that delighted me. He set me to reading the Spectator; and it was then that I acquired my first notions of taste for the fine arts and of the pleasure there is in considering the variety of human nature. I read the Roman poets, and I felt a classic enthusiasm in the romantic shades of our family's seat in the country. My governor sometimes spoke to me of religion, but in a simple and pleasing way. He told me that if I behaved well during my life, I should be happy in the other world. There I should hear beautiful music. There I should acquire the sublime knowledge that God will grant to the righteous; and there I should meet all the great men of whom I had read, and all the dear friends I had known. At last my governor put me in love with Heaven, and some hope entered into my religion.*

When Boswell reached the age of twelve, Dun was replaced by another tutor of whom he had a lower opinion. He describes him as

> *a very honest man but harsh and without knowledge of the human mind... He had no other idea than to make me perform a task. When I asked him questions about the poets, for instruction or amusement – and why should I not have looked for amusement? – he*

lost his temper and cried out with a schoolmaster's arrogance,
'Come, come, keep at work, don't interrupt the lesson. Time is flying.'
Consequently, I got the habit of reading without any profit. It was
enough to say that I had read such and such an author.

There we have a delightful pen picture of the young Boswell in the schoolroom, already demonstrating an independence of mind.

In the main, however, family life was based in Edinburgh. The young James preferred town to country life and would be pleased to be off after a stay at Auchinleck. Let us, in the mind's eye, travel with the family over the Lanarkshire hills, through the seemingly endless miles of heather and bog, on the two-day journey back to the city. Until suddenly, and from afar, the towers and 'reek' of Scotland's ancient capital appear on the black ridge that rises above the Forth.

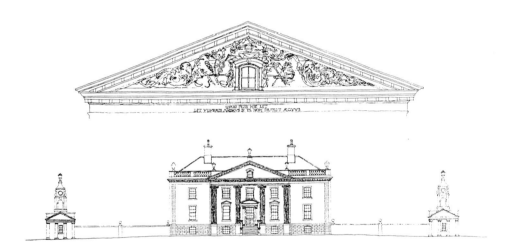

Auchinleck House
East Elevation

CHAPTER 2

Edinburgh
and the
Early Years:
1740 – 1760

The Edinburgh of Boswell's youth was about to expand dramatically. From time immemorial, the city had occupied the narrow, sloping ridge of land that runs from the ancient castle on its rock down to the Palace of Holyrood. In fact, it is more accurate to say that the ancient city had occupied about half of that mile-long slope. Beneath the Netherbow Port, halfway down the hill, the city became the burgh of the Canongate. This was more than a notional distinction, for a different set of local laws and privileges attached to each community. For this reason, and perhaps for reasons of security, the burgesses and town-folk of Edinburgh had clung to the upper reach of the settlement, rendering it progressively overcrowded.

The first overall picture we have of the old city is that provided by the

The Royal Palace of Holyrood House.

Holyrood House, c. 1750 by Foundrinier, from Maitland's *History of Edinburgh*.

excellent bird's-eye view plan of 1647 by Gordon of Rothiemay. There is the Old Town still crammed into its late medieval site, bounded on the north by the Nor' Loch and to the south by the Burgh Loch. There can be seen, in admirable detail, the then newly erected Parliament House, the ancient Tolbooth and the crazy old streets and closes that Boswell would run about in as a boy. The old city was dominated by the great bulk of the castle. In turbulent times, its doors would close to secure the fastness for whatever faction then held it. The last half-hearted siege of the castle took place when Edinburgh was temporarily occupied by the Jacobite forces of the Young Pretender in September and October of 1745. The government troops in the castle were the only forces in the city actively to oppose the Prince's army. An occasional cannonball is said to have whizzed down the High Street, to the consternation of the populace. It is likely that young James Boswell would then be safely at his grandfather's home at Auchinleck, as the Court of Session did not sit that winter on account of the unrest caused by the Rebellion. It may be, though, that the youngster did see something of the later stages of the campaign. While on his travels in Germany in 1764, he amused himself by penning in his journal a reminiscence of the last contact he had had with German troops:

> *Behold, ye Hessians, from the Shire of Ayr,*
> *A laird whom your moustaches have made stare:*
> *While a mere child, not yet advanced to taw [marbles]*
> *You in Edina's ancient town he saw,*
> *When the Rebellion you came o'er to quell*
> *And send forsooth, the monster back to Hell;*
> *While Arthur's Seat resounded with your drums,*
> *I saw you buying breeches for your bums;*
> *But, with your breeches, you were not so stout*
> *As the bold Highlanders who went without.*

Boswell's childhood also coincided with the appearance of the first detailed account of the city. William Maitland published his *History of Edinburgh* in 1753. The work promised to give: 'A Faithful Relation of the publick Transactions of the Citizens; Accounts of the several Parishes; its Governments, Civil, Ecclesiastical, and Military; Incorporation of Trades and Manufactures; Courts of Justice; State of Learning; Charitable Foundations, etc.'. In fact, the work was very comprehensive and gives an excellent picture of the city, still within its old confines. Best of all, it includes the first accurate plan of the capital as it was in 1742. Drawn up by William Edgar, 'Architect', and said to have been two years in the making, the plan shows the whole length of the town from castle to palace, with its multiplicity of closes, or alleys, tumbling down the two sides of the ridge to the north and south. By curious coincidence, a later legal dispute involving Edgar's heirs, in a claim against Maitland for his use and retention of the plan, had Boswell's father as counsel for the heirs.

Maitland attempts to calculate the population of Edinburgh at the time of his work. By reference to the computed number of houses in the city (and reckoning five and a half occupants per house!) as well as reference to the records of burials over a period of years, Maitland calculated the population at just over 50,000. In a slightly later survey (1755), Boswell's uncle by marriage, the Rev Alexander Webster, computed more than 31,000 in the city, plus at least 12,000 in the adjoining St Cuthbert's parish. In a modern study of Edinburgh as it was in 1752, James Gilhooley puts the figure for the Old Town population at about 23,500. Whatever the exact number, in the 1750s Edinburgh was bursting at the seams. After a

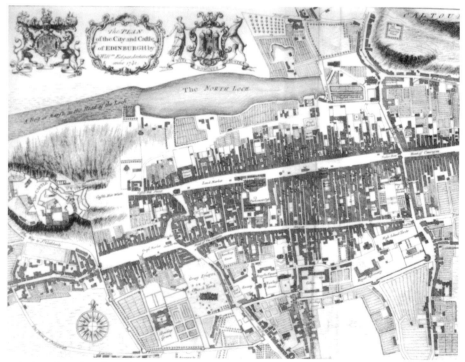

Edinburgh 1742: The Old City as mapped by William Edgar.

A Perspective View of the Front of the Tron Kirk with the Adjoining Buildings.

Edinburgh in the late 18th century. The High Street and Tron Kirk (from Arnot's *History of Edinburgh*).

survey of the city, and a calculation that the total of its various thoroughfares was 329, Maitland had this to say on the subject:

> *The great number of streets, squares, courts, wynds, closes and rows abovementioned to be in a place of so small dimensions such as Edinburgh is, will, no doubt, surprise the citizens themselves; wherefore, it is necessary to observe, that the closes or alleys in the principal streets are so very numerous, that there is seldom more than one row of buildings between two closes and those so very high and crowded with people, that the great number of inhabitants of the city will presently appear to be as amazing as the said great number of streets, squares, etc. wherein are contained 9,064 houses…*

One of the difficulties he had in conducting a census of the population was that:

> *in the months of July, August and September, in the dead time of the vacation… a number of the inhabitants… retire into the country at this season either for pleasure or profit, many of them leave their houses in town with only one servant to look after them respectively; others have not half the family; nay, some of them are left without any person to take care of them. But the greatest defect, is owing to the Episcopalian inhabitants, who, being of a different communion from the established church, are not subject to the control and examination of its ministers; wherefore many of them refuse to give accounts either of the names or numbers of persons in their families.*

These facts are also mentioned because it was in just such a vacation, only a few years after this was written, that the young James Boswell took the opportunity of his parents' absence to acquaint himself with the Episcopalian religion.

As Maitland wrote his work, schemes for improvement of the city were afoot. On 8 July 1752 (our James would be about twelve), the Convention of Royal Burghs of Scotland resolved to publish *Proposals for carrying on certain Public Works in the City of Edinburgh*. In its preface to the proposals, the report compares Edinburgh unfavourably with London:

> *To illustrate this further, we need only contrast the delightful prospect which London affords, with that of any other city which is destitute of all, or even of any considerable number of these advantages. Sorry we are, but no-one occurs to us more apposite to this purpose, than Edinburgh, the metropolis of Scotland when a separate kingdom, and still the chief city of North Britain. The healthfulness of its situation, and its neighbourhood to the Forth, must no doubt be admitted as very favourable circumstances. But how greatly are these over-balanced by other disadvantages almost without number? Placed upon the ridge of a hill, it admits but of one good street, running from East to West; and even this is tolerably accessible only from one quarter. The narrow lanes leading to the North and South, by reason of their steepness, narrowness and dirtiness, can only be considered so many unavoidable nuisances. Confined by the small compass of the walls, and the narrow limits of the Royalty which scarcely extends beyond the walls, the houses stand more crowded than in any other town in Europe, and are built to a height which is almost incredible. Hence necessarily follows a great want of free air, light, cleanliness, and every other comfortable accommodation. Hence also many families, sometimes no less than ten or a dozen, are obliged to live overhead of each other in the same building: where, to all the other inconveniencies, is added that of a common stair, which is no other in effect than an upright street, constantly dark and dirty. It is owing to the same narrowness of situation, that the principal street is incumbered with the herb-market, the fruit market, and several others; that the shambles are placed on the side of the North-Loch rendering what was originally an ornament to the town, a most insufferable nuisance. No less observable is the great deficiency of public buildings. If the Parliament House, the churches*

*and a few hospital s be excepted, what other do we have to boast of?
There is no exchange for our merchants; no safe repository for our
public and private records; no place of meeting for our magistrates
and town council; none for the Convention of our Burghs, which is
entrusted with the inspection of trade. To these and such other
reasons it must be imputed, that so few people of rank reside in the
city; that it is rarely visited by strangers; and that so many local
prejudices, and narrow notions, inconsistent with the polished
manners and growing wealth, are still so obstinately retained. To
such reasons alone it must be imputed that Edinburgh, which ought
to have set the first example of industry and improvement, is the last
of our trading cities that has shook off the unaccountable supineness
which has so long and so fatally depressed the spirit of this nation.*

Strong stuff indeed and just as well to have been written by Scotsmen, one
feels!

The *'Proposals'* go on to note the existence of 'a truly public and
national spirit' for improvement and a remarkable advance in the
industries and enterprises of the nation since the suppression of the
Rebellion in 1746.

*The meanness of Edinburgh has been too long an obstruction to our
improvement, and a reproach to Scotland. The increase of our
people, the extension of our commerce, and the honour of the
nation, are all concerned in the success of this project. As we have
such powerful motives prompting us to undertake it; so chance has
furnished us with the fairest opportunity of carrying it into
execution. Several of the principal parts of the town are now lying in
ruins. Many of the old houses are decayed; several have already
been pulled down, and probably more will soon be in the same
condition. If this opportunity be neglected, all hopes of remedying the
inconveniencies of this city are at an end.*

After some twenty-five pages of preamble, the report eventually comes to
the point and proposes:

1. *To build upon the ruins on the north side of the High Street, an
   exchange with proper accommodations for our merchants.*
2. *To erect upon the ruins in the Parliament Close, a large*

building, containing such accommodations as are still wanting
for the Courts of Justice, the Royal Burghs, and Town Council,
offices for the clerks, proper apartments for the several registers,
and for the Advocates Library.

3. *To obtain an act of parliament for extending the Royalty; to*
   enlarge and beautify the town by opening new streets to the
   north and south, removing the markets and shambles, and
   turning the North Loch into a canal, with walks and terrasses on
   each side.
4. *That the expense of these public works should be defrayed by a*
   national contribution.

That these proposals were very forward-looking cannot be denied. The implementation of the third in particular was to revolutionise the layout of Edinburgh within seventy-five years. A reservation is expressed:

that this project may occasion the centre of the town to be deserted.
But of this there can be no hazard. People of fortune, and of a
certain rank, will probably chuse to build upon the fine fields which
lie to the north and south of the town: but men of professions and
business of every kind, will still incline to live in the neighbourhood
of the Exchange, of the Courts of Justice and other places of public
resort; and the number of this last class of men will increase in a
much greater proportion, than that of the former.

And, on a note pertinent to the Boswellian theme, the authors observed:

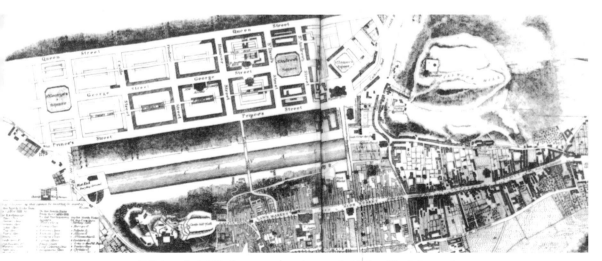

Edinburgh, 1780, the spread to the north (John Ainslie's map).

'Let us improve and enlarge the city, and possibly the superior pleasures of London, which is at a distance, will be compensated, at least in some measure, by the moderate pleasures of Edinburgh, which is at home.' There is a distinct pre-echo here of the sentiment to be expressed by Lord Auchinleck on the pediment of the new Auchinleck House. One wonders if he had a hand in the drafting of the document, appearing as he does as one of the directors of the proposals, nominated by the Faculty of Advocates.

The spirit of improvement was to dominate civic life in Edinburgh throughout the period of Boswell's life. Such was its pace that the city frequently became financially embarrassed by the cost and scale of the enterprise. None the less, by 1771 David Hume, the historian and philosopher, could move himself from James Court in the Old Town to St Andrew's Square in the New, Boswell and his family coincidentally leasing his old flat. In 1772 the North Bridge connecting the Old and New Town was opened. And in June 1774 Boswell attended the ceremony of the laying of the foundation stone of Register House, the magnificent new home for the Registers of Scotland designed by Robert Adam. A new 'Exchange' was in fact completed in 1761, but the merchants, perhaps not relishing the expense of their proposed contribution, decided against their

Old Edinburgh: the view down the High Street from the Lawnmarket.

Old Edinburgh :
the West Bow before
improvement (from Storer's
Views 1820).

new home and the handsome building off the High Street was eventually
taken over by the town council and remains to this day the headquarters of
the municipal authority. Of the building proposals, only those for the
Advocates Library remained unexecuted. Although extensions to the
library were built throughout the nineteenth century (at the expense of the
Faculty), the basic accommodation for the books remained in the old Laigh
Hall of the Parliament House until the National Library was completed in
1956, to store that part of the collection gifted to the nation by the Faculty
in 1925.

For Boswell as a boy, then, his Edinburgh was the old, as yet
unimproved city. He was born on 29 October 1740 in his father's home on
the fourth storey of an old tenement, Blair's Land, in Parliament Close. This
complex of buildings, grouped to the south of St Giles in the High Street,

A surviving fragment of the old West Bow.

occupied roughly the site of the present-day Parliament Square (Lord Cockburn decried as 'foppery', the fashion whereby the name was prettified). The west side of the close, as can be seen from Edgar's map was, and still is, occupied by the Parliament House. To the south, the ground falls away very steeply down to the Cowgate. Both the Fish Market and Meal Market were in the immediate proximity. Steep wynds or stairs ran down to these. Because of the fall in the ground, the front of the tenements or lands forming the square would be perhaps four storeys high but, to the rear, the buildings would rise up to eight or nine storeys above the lower street. With the resultant warren of wynds and closes, the potential fire risk was always great. Up and down the High Street, disastrous fires broke out from time to time. Finally, in the most disastrous of a series of fires in 1824 (sketched by Turner amongst others), the whole of the east side of Parliament Close was destroyed, including the old Boswell family home. Then the spirit of improvement took over, and there were erected in the early years of the nineteenth century, to Lord Cockburn's disgust, 'the bright freestone and contemptible decorations' which now form the screen to the square.

As a lad James Boswell would be well used to running up and down dark stairs and malodorous closes. He describes himself as scurrying home from school: 'down the Horse Wynd, up Borthwicks Close . . . by the crowded Cross, regardless of advocates, writers, Scotch Hunters, cloth merchants, Presbyterian ministers, country lairds, captains both by land and sea, porters, chairmen and cadies'. Boswell then goes on to describe the agonies of impatience with which he waited for dinner to be set on the table and for his tutor, Mr Ferguson, to finish his ample benedictions. 'Then did I mightily fall on, and make a meal most prodigious.'

The Mr Ferguson mentioned we have already come across as the successor to James's first tutor, the Rev John Dun. Prior to this, the young Boswell had spent two years or so undergoing more formal schooling at the private academy of James Mundell in the West Bow, which he first attended aged six. The West Bow is one of the parts of Old Edinburgh largely swept away by mid-nineteenth-century improvements. It formerly took a twisting, precipitous course from the head of the High Street (Lawnmarket) to the Grassmarket, 100 feet or so beneath. Its z-shaped course can be plainly seen on Edgar's map. Even today, vestiges of the street remain. One can see where it formerly started its descent (Bow Head) and where it debouched into the Grassmarket, just at the old place of execution. Some of the original houses still stand, as at the south-west corner of Victoria Street which cut a swathe through the old quarter in the 1830s. To descend the headlong flight of steps that now connects the upper fragment with the lower gives a good impression of how steep this entrance to the western part of the Old Town must have been. In his *Traditions of Edinburgh* (originally published in 1823), Robert Chambers described the West Bow as a 'curious, angular, whimsical looking street of great steepness and narrowness', and then goes on to devote a whole chapter to its characters and traditions. One of these concerned the infamous Major Weir, said to have been in league with the Devil, and burned in 1670 for crimes against nature and his sister. For years his old house was reputedly haunted and was a place of terror and dare-devilry for passing schoolboys. The young James describes himself as a nervous and superstitious child: ' Afraid of the cold and everything else. A complete poltroon in the streets of Edinburgh.' Such legends and imaginary terrors (so proximate to the real ones at the foot of the street) could not have helped.

After his short time at Mundell's, young Boswell was educated at home, either in the city or at Auchinleck. It is clear that he supplemented the more stolid educational fare that his tutors fed him with such lighter materials as he could find. The *Spectator,* for example, is said to have early whetted his appetite for London life.

The next stage of Boswell's education commenced in 1753 when, at the age of thirteen, he was enrolled at the University or College of Edinburgh. In common with many of the other young students (Sir Walter Scott started such classes some years later aged twelve), he then embarked on the general arts course, which included Latin, Greek, logic and philosophy. Until recent times, a general arts course in Scotland was regarded as a desirable precursor to a more specialised professional degree. Given the age of many of the students and one suspects, the standard of some of the teaching, such an initial course was more akin to what we would regard nowadays as secondary education. Nonetheless, the standards of literacy were high. There is an early family letter from the thirteen-year-old James to his mother (17 July 1754), which is in excellent English. Moreover, the young students would be expected to have a working knowledge of Latin and Greek. With a reputed classical scholar for a father, it would have been surprising if Boswell had not been a good Latinist. He was thereby to facilitate his learning of modern languages both at home and abroad. On his Tour, he was able to express himself in German and Italian. He could speak French fluently and apparently without shame to Rousseau and Voltaire. The terrors of the West Bow and the later freezing winter excursions down to the Old College were not to be in vain.

It should not be imagined that the college of Boswell's day bore any resemblance to the massive, elegant building which now houses the Old Quadrangle. In the 1750's, the university occupied a picturesque jumble of ancient buildings, clearly ripe for redevelopment. William Robertson, the historian, who was to become a distinguished Principal of the college in 1762, described the state of the buildings in 1768 thus:

A stranger when conducted to view the university of Edinburgh,
might on seeing such courts and buildings, naturally enough
imagine them to be almshouses for the reception of the poor; but
would never imagine he was entering within the precincts of a noted
and flourishing seat of learning. An area, which, if entire, would
have formed one spacious quadrangle, is broken into three paltry
divisions, and encompassed partly with walls which threaten
destruction to the passenger, and partly with a range of low houses,
several of which are now become ruinous and not habitable. With
the exception of one large upper gallery, which has lately been
repaired and made the Public Library, and of an anatomical
theatre, there is no room or building belonging to the university that

has any degree of academical decency. The teaching rooms of the professors are, in general, mean, straitened, and inconvenient; and some professors, whose hours of teaching follow immediately on one another, are obliged to occupy the same rooms.

The university had no accommodation for students, but the Boswell home in Parliament Close was just a few minutes away. To complete the picture, it has to be recollected that the South Bridge, fronting the present university buildings, was not completed until 1788. The approach to the college would be up from the Cowgate by College Wynd, or from one of the other narrow streets that then ran alongside the old building.

The golden days of Edinburgh Enlightenment scholarship under Robertson, Adam Ferguson, Dugald Stewart, Hugh Blair and Baron Hume, the lawyer, were still some years ahead. None-the-less, Boswell appears to have benefited from his courses of lectures; particularly those given by John Stevenson on logic and metaphysics. These were geared to stir the imagination of the student. With Boswell, it appears that the teaching aim

The entrance to James Court, from the Lawnmarket, Edinburgh.

may have succeeded too well. The youngster seems to have been constantly plagued with religious and sexual misgivings. On two occasions his health broke down and he had to be sent off to Moffat to recover his equilibrium and physical health. At this stage (aged about fifteen), he is said to have been 'a thick set boy, inclining to plumpness, physically very robust and active, with black hair and eyes and a very dark complexion'. He was about five feet six inches in stature. The earliest portrait which we have of the young James was painted some years later in Rome when he was about twenty-four. The portrait of the young Boswell sitting in his finery bears out the description (see frontispiece).

As he grew older, Boswell's confidence increased. It was from about this time that his cheerful and boisterous demeanour became apparent to others. People were either charmed or repelled by Boswell. And it has to be said that the majority of people were charmed. One of the striking characteristics of the young man was his ability to ingratiate himself with both the higher and lower orders of society. He was able to gain entrée to the hermit philosopher Rousseau. He was also able to bed his housekeeper. But always in the background there was the lurking 'black dog' of depression to which Boswell was highly prone. He was also fearful of the history of mental illness that was a trait of his family, and to which his own younger brother John was to fall victim. A complex and outgoing young man, then, subject to fears and foibles, but with distinct social and literary gifts.

From about this time, Boswell starts to speak for himself. Throughout his life Boswell was a great journalist (in both senses), pamphleteer and correspondent. In his late teens, he commenced two important courses of letter writing, which give us detailed insight into his thoughts and activities. The first of Boswell's correspondents was his fellow student William Temple. A year or so older than Boswell, Temple was eventually to become an English clergyman. He shared Boswell's literary interests and eventually made a minor name for himself. He also became increasingly frustrated at the shortcomings of a parson's country life, particularly since it was encumbered by a family of at least eight children! Temple was much more of a puritan than Boswell. The latter, from an early stage, seems to have taken a delight in treating Temple as a confessor figure – albeit by correspondence. Despite the manifest differences in their characters, Boswell and Temple remained friends and correspondents until Boswell's death in 1795. The other friend who appears about this time is John Johnston – not to be confused with the great Dr Johnson, who Boswell

David Hume (1711 - 76):
philosopher and historian.
Friend of the Young Boswell.
Portrait by Allan Ramsay.

had still to meet. Johnston was Laird of Grange, a small estate in Dumfriesshire. Although taking classes at the same time as Boswell and Temple, Johnston, or 'Grange', as Boswell often refers to him, appears to have been in his middle twenties. Said to have been convivial, he may well have introduced the young Boswell to some of the pleasures of the tavern and the theatre. Again, this friendship was to be of long standing. Much of our knowledge of Boswell's activities during his European travels comes from the many letters he wrote to Johnston. At the time of Johnston's death in 1786, Boswell referred to him as 'my oldest friend, Grange'.

At the time under discussion, however, the three friends were young, lively men. Surviving early letters provide some fascinating details. In July 1758, for example, Boswell wrote to Temple about his having been introduced to the famous philosopher and historian, David Hume. Hume at this time was forty-seven years old and resident in Edinburgh.

Some days ago, I was introduced to your friend Mr Hume; he is a most discreet, affable man as ever I met with, and has really a great deal of learning, and a choice collection of books. He is indeed an

extraordinary man – few such people are to be met with nowadays.
We talk a great deal of genius, fine language, improving our style,
etc. but I am afraid solid learning is much wore out. Mr Hume, I
think, is a very proper person for a young man to cultivate an
acquaintance with. Though he has perhaps the most delicate taste,
yet he has applied himself with great attention to the study of the
ancients, and is likewise a great historian, so that you are not only
entertained in his company, but may reap a great deal of useful
instruction. I own myself much obliged to you, dear sir, for
procuring me the pleasure of his acquaintance.

Some of this, one feels, might have been written with the Boswellian tongue in the cheek, since Hume already had a scandalous reputation for atheism and free-thinking. Only the year before, he had resigned his post as librarian of the Advocates Library over a dispute with the curators as to whether or not French novels were to be purchased. Throughout his life Boswell was to have a penchant for dangerous friends (John Wilkes springs to mind).

In the same letter, Boswell reports a budding (but fruitless) romance with a Miss Whyte, the first of a long series of such confessions. Later that year, he reports that he has been on circuit with his father and Sir David Dalrymple (the future Lord Hailes). He continues: 'I kept an exact journal at the particular desire of my friend Mr Love and sent it to him in sheets every post.' This is interesting on two counts. It is the first record we have of Boswell keeping a journal. Secondly, Love, an actor, appears to have given him an introduction to the world of actors while, later, his wife was to be Boswell's mistress.

To Johnston, he writes from Auchinleck, in September 1759: 'Auchinleck is a most sweet romantic place. There is a vast deal of wood and water, fine retired shady walks and everything that can render the country agreeable to contemplative minds.' Again, echoes of the sentiment on the pediment of his father's new house. And, in a letter of 27 August 1762, he reports that he is 'now in the new house, where I have a neat elegant apartment, which contributes to render me cheerful and well'. But this is to anticipate. Much of his chatter to Johnston is of 'theatrical news'. The eighteen-year-old Boswell had fallen in love with actors and an actress.

In the Edinburgh of 1759 the theatre had a very tenuous position. The prevalent Presbyterian attitude of the townspeople was to regard the theatre and its frequenters as the works of the Devil and the damned respectively. Nonetheless, a group of actors had acquired theatre premises at the head of the Canongate and various plays were staged. With typical enthusiasm for his new-found passion, Boswell appears to have contributed reviews of the plays to a local newspaper, the *Edinburgh Chronicle*. Not content with that, he seems to have made arrangements for the same to be published in booklet form as *A View of the Edinburgh Theatre During the Summer Season 1759*. Claiming to be 'By A Society of Gentlemen', the pamphlet is thought to be in fact Boswell's first publication. An internal clue is the extravagant praise given throughout to an actress, one Mrs Cowper. She is variously described as having 'the finest person, the most agreeable face, and the politest character of any actress we remember to have seen on this stage'; as being 'our favourite actress … entirely the woman of Quality… her Elegance of dress and Graceful behaviour convinced us of her being able to shine with becoming Lustre in the Drawing-room', and so on. The lady in question is thought to have been several years older than her admirer and to have blighted her own social chances by marrying her music master. She is unlikely to have been other than kind to the young Boswell.

Less kind was Lord Auchinleck when he learned of his son's gallivantings during the summer vacation. After what must have been a terse interview with his father, the nineteen-year-old Boswell was despatched to Glasgow University to pursue his studies. To Johnston he writes (11 January 1760):

> *'I dare say you would be greatly surprised on hearing that I was come hither as the result of an unexpected decision of my father in whose judgement it became wise for me to leave Edinburgh. I must confess that it made me not a little uneasy at first, to think of being deprived of the happiness I usually enjoyed, and hoped for this winter, in my good friends and acquaintances at Edinburgh, but I resolved to bring my mind to be contented with the situation which was thought proper for me.*

At this stage, though, he seems to have been prepared to make the best of his situation and continues:

> *My greatest inducement for coming hither was to hear Mr Smith's lectures which are truly excellent. His Sentiments are striking*

*profound and beautiful, the method in which they are arranged
clear, accurate and orderly; his language correct perspicuous and
elegantly phrased. His private character is really amiable. He has
nothing of that formal stiffness and Pedantary which is too often
found in professors. So far from that, he is a most polite well bred
man, is extremely fond of having his students with him and treats
them with all the easiness and affability imaginable.*

The Mr Smith mentioned was of course the famous Adam Smith, the future
author of *The Wealth of Nations* (1776). Smith was then Professor of Moral
Philosophy at the university and Boswell also attended his lectures on
rhetoric and belles-lettres. Smith seems to have been friendly towards his
students and, in a letter, commended Boswell on his 'happy facility of
manners'. It may also have been Smith who first alerted the potential
biographer of Dr Johnson to the value of minutiae in recreating the person
and habits of a subject.

But compared to Edinburgh, Glasgow in 1760 was a prosaic place. No
doubt the inhabitants could be described as 'very rich, saucy and wicked',
as they were by the English traveller Sarah Murray some years later. But of
public entertainments and diversions there were then few. For the
ebullient (presumed) author of the *View of the Edinburgh Theatre* which
had appeared in February of 1760, the situation rapidly became
intolerable.

The next development in the career of the young Boswell was a truly
dramatic one.

CHAPTER 3

The Young Adult:
1760 – 1762

On 1 March 1760, the nineteen-year-old James Boswell took horse and bolted for London. Although the emphasis in the present work is on Boswell's life in its Scottish context, some account has to be given, and taken, of events elsewhere; particularly where significant in the make-up of the man he was becoming.

However distressing the sudden turn of events must have been for Boswell's parents, they cannot have been entirely surprised that something of the sort had happened. From about the age of fifteen, Boswell had often expressed a desire to be a soldier and to fight in the wars then current in Europe and North America. The times, after all, were stirring ones. For some years, too, Boswell had been going through the sort of religious crisis that one often sees in thinking adolescents. Under the influence of Temple he had attended an Episcopalian service while still in Edinburgh. He was, and always would be, attracted to ceremony and ritual. No doubt too his contact with the English actors and actresses in the summer of 1759 had made him question the dour discipline of Presbyterianism. Most significant, the actress amorata, Mrs Cowper, was a Roman Catholic. She had put the young Boswell in touch with her priest who had given him instructive Catholic literature. The young James had even announced to Lord Auchinleck his intention to become a convert. No doubt these developments had persuaded the father that Boswell should not return to such influences in Edinburgh. To become a Catholic in eighteenth-century Edinburgh would be to render oneself politically suspect and professionally ineligible for office. A crisis had clearly been brewing, and now the storm had broken.

For once we have no Boswell to guide us through the momentous events that followed. The well-known *London Journal* is a record of his next trip to the metropolis, prior to his studying and touring in Europe in the early 1760s. Professor Pottle remarks that the first sojourn in London was one of the few episodes in his life about which Boswell 'remained at all times secretive'. One wonders whether perhaps there may remain another, as yet undiscovered journal, dealing with the adventure. As we know, Boswell was already journalising. It seems incredible that he would not have kept some record of the most significant period in his life to date. Not all of his papers have survived of course. Even the *London Journal* only came to light in 1928. Perhaps in an attic somewhere, or deep in the archives of a family with Boswell connections, there yet remains an account of the whirlwind and intriguing three months spent in the capital.

In outline, then, Boswell rode to London with very little money. He stayed in town, at first incognito. He simultaneously put himself in touch with both Roman Catholics and friends in the world of theatre. He was inducted not only into the Roman Catholic Church, but also into the 'melting and transporting rites of love' within the first three weeks of his arrival. He had also by then renewed contact with his father. Lord Auchinleck asked a nobleman neighbour and friend, Lord Eglinton, to assist. The latter had Boswell traced and took the young man under his wing. The wing was a rakish one and the Earl made it his business to convince Boswell that there was more to life than either the religious way or that of the soldier. He introduced the nineteen-year-old into the London high society of the time. He met the heir presumptive to the throne, the young Duke of York. The encounter later inspired some bad verse:

The Royal Youth has ask'd me gay;
Come, Boswell, what have you to say … [etc].

In short, at the price of his fledgling principles, Boswell was convinced that he should co-operate with his father and family, at least in the meantime, and continue his studies in Scotland. Lord Auchinleck himself came to town to collect his errant son and, apparently reconciled, they went north together again.

The state of reconciliation did not last long. Boswell had agreed to study at home, with a view to passing advocate in due course. However, the alternative strategy of his obtaining a commission in the Guards or some other old, honourable regiment was never far from his mind. In the meantime depending on where the household was, he either moped (and studied) at Auchinleck or socialised in Edinburgh. The mood is summarised in a letter to Temple written in the following May (1761):

> *I grant you that my behaviour has not been entirely as it ought to be. A young fellow whose happiness was always centred in London, who had at least got there, and had begun to taste its delights, who had got his mind filled with the most gay ideas – getting into the Guards, being about Court, enjoying the happiness of the beau monde and the company of men of genius, in short everything that he did wish – consider this poor fellow hauled away to the town of Edinburgh, obliged to conform to every Scotch custom or be laughed at – 'Will ye hae some jeel? oh fie! oh fie!' – his flighty imagination quite cramped, and he obliged to study Corpus Juris Civilis, and live in his father's strict family; is there any wonder, sir, that the unlucky dog should be somewhat fretful? Yoke a Newmarket courser to a dung-cart, and I'll lay my life on't he'll either caper and kick most confoundedly, or be as stupid and restive as an old, battered post horse. Not one in a hundred can understand this; you do.*

All was far from hard work however. A few days after he wrote this letter, Boswell was off on the Northern Circuit with his father. A short journal of the trip to Inverness exists at Yale, the first of his journals to survive. And there was to be a much more extensive and ambitious journey through south-west Scotland the following autumn.

Despite all his good resolutions, Boswell's life at this stage was far from dull.

As soon as James returned to Edinburgh he took up his former connection with the theatre. He also threw himself into literary endeavours of a more or less juvenile cast. He wrote poems, pamphlets, letters (serious and frivolous), reviews and burlesques. The chief value in these occasional and ephemeral pieces is the light that they throw on Boswell's development as author and adult. Scattered as they are throughout the multifarious popular publications of the day, the identification of the authorship of such pieces involves literary detective work of the most devoted kind. The major work in this field is Professor Pottle's *Literary Career of James Boswell, Esq.*, originally published in 1929. That Pottle was able to pore through the files of the *Scots, London, Gentleman's* and *European* magazines from 1758 onwards and identify pieces by the

The fiend seems smiling at the work of death,
  And hears, with pleasure hears, the murder-
    er's voice:
When lo! at once, Fear's dreadful pow'r is felt,
  As injur'd Banquo points the livid wound,
Cold chilling dews upon his forehead melt,
  Fades the gay scene of splendor all around,
Drops from his nerveless hand the rosy bowl,
While sluggish through his veins life's purple tor-
    rents roll.

VII.
And mark where Richard, near his tent,
  Tastes the cool fragrance of the air,
Remorse within his bosom pent,
  And deadly Hate, and black Despair;
Yet once again, behold, he sleeps,
Hark! on his ear the low groan creeps;
He shudd'ring starts, convulsive shakes,
He heaves, he turns, he leaps, he wakes;
Each feature seems with wild amazement hung,
The sudden pray'r to Heav'n drops falt'ring from
    his tongue.

VIII.
Shakespeare alone thy ghastly charms enjoy'd,
  Thy savage haunts he travers'd undismay'd,
In hearing thy awak'ning tales employ'd,
  Where the wood darkens to a deeper shade;
And if I read the magic page aright,
Loud thunders roll'd around th'enchanted spot,
While fire-ey'd dæmons growl'd the long lone
    night,
And ev'ry tree with flashing flame was smote;
And cries uncouth, and sounds of wo were heard,
And tall gigantic shapes their horrid forms up-
    rear'd.

IX.
But not alone to guilt confin'd,
  Thy furies dart their secret stings,
They point them at the virtuous mind,
  Which each ideal fancy wings:
The pensive melancholy Dane
Deep mourns his royal father slain;
Th'unnatural murderer must bleed,
The ghost appears, and prompts the deed;
Even valiant Brutus, sinking to repose,
Thy awful presence felt as his stern genius rose.

X.
Ye angels sent as guardians of the good,
  Swift chase th'enthusiastic pow'r away,
Clear the low cloud, each grief-charg'd thought
    exclude,
Drive hence the fiend that shuns the eye of day;
Ah! calm and gentle sink us down to rest
Let Chearfulness the lonely void adorn,
Let her mild radiance gild the fear-struck breast,
While we with air-form'd terrors cease tomourn;
And in such raptur'd dreams the fancy steep,
As render more endear'd the deity of Sleep.

Extempore, by a Win———ter scholar,
    On reading a North Briton.

Go on, dear W———s, go on and write,
  Nor fear the lack of matter;
Each black-guard claims it as his right,
  His betters to bespatter.

ODE. By James Boswell, Esq;
On an engagement between the Rt Hon. Lady
    B****, and a Turky-Cock.

I.
Swell, swell, the mighty song,
Let strains exhalted rend the trembling air;
  The great atchievements of the fair
    Deserve poetic fire!
Such as sublimely blaz'd around,
When at the elevating sound
    Of lofty Pindar's lyre,
Astonish'd stood th'attentive Grecian throng.

II.
Th'Olympic games of old
Ne'er saw such resolution bold.
  The Amazonian train,
Could they, recall'd to life, but see,
O dame, the valiant deeds, to thee
  Would own their prowess vain;
In vain were they, as soon as born,
Doom'd by their mothers fell, to mourn
The female comeliness of breast
By the knife's cruel edge opprest;
When Lady B——— can deride
Their feeble far inferior power,
In horrid conflict's trying hour,
And yet retain her bosom's snowy pride.

III.
See the imperious Turky-Cock,
  Of size like Ardven's rock!
See him in rage advance,   [France!
Like Marischal Turenne, the warlike boast of
See! how he proudly treads the ground,
  Looking with fierce disdain;
His varied feathers ruffling all around,
While scarlet ire his head and neck does stain.
His wings extended wide the pavement brush,
  As on he comes with hideous rush:
His chest sends forth a sounding hum;
As from the hollow womb of unbrac'd drum:
Or, like the twang of smoaking cord
  Fix'd to the bow of yew,
Which ancient Caledonian Lord,
Or chieftain much renown'd, in bloody battle
    drew.

IV.
But lo! with grand majestic mien
Her handsome Ladyship is seen
In rich blue satin robe array'd,
The colour that can never fade:
Not lovelier could Malvina seem,   [grace,
When in her hunting vestment, cloath'd with
By Lora's sweetly murmuring stream,
She wander'd eager for the sportive chace:
  In her smooth alabaster hand
  She grasps an oaken wand,
And now, Approach, thou furious vaunting bird!
Through all the circling air is loudly heard.

V.
The youthful family in haste
  To all the windows fly;
While Andrew, bless'd with genius and with taste,
Shoots glances wild from either eye,

G g 2   Just

An early *Ode by James Boswell Esq.* from the *Scots Magazine* of April 1763.

youthful journalist must excite the greatest admiration. Less obscure was a publication comprising a *Collection of Poems by Scotch Gentlemen*, published in February 1762 by Alexander Donaldson (father of the publisher Donaldson who founded the still-existing school for the deaf in Edinburgh). Boswell and his friend Andrew Erskine contributed several poems to this collection. Some of them are quite cheerful but none is of any great merit.

Needless to say, the contemporary reception of some of these works was sometimes less than ecstatic. By his 'Letter from a Gentleman of Scotland to the Earl of… in London' *(Scots Magazine,* September, 1761), Boswell managed to alienate his former patron Lord Eglinton. And by his sheer presumption in publishing the *Cub at Newmarket* (London, March 1762) with an unauthorised dedication to the Duke of York, he further angered the nobleman who had taken such trouble with the young runaway two years before. A series of letters between himself and his friend Erskine was also published, at Boswell's insistence, in April 1763. Again, indiscretions were rife. Lord Auchinleck commented wearily: 'Though it might pass between two intimate young lads in the same way that people over a bottle will be vastly entertained with one another's rant, it was extremely odd to send such a piece to the press to be perused by all and sundry.' The father concluded that he should 'do what you can to make me happy, in place of striving, as it were, to find out the things… most galling to me and making these your pursuit'. This impulsive way of proceeding was to characterise Boswell in years to come and was effectively to deny him public office and professional advancement.

Boswell could impress both as a sober and talented young man, and as a facetious rake. David Hume thought highly of him and described him to a French correspondent in 1766 as 'a friend of mine, a young gentleman, very good humoured, very agreeable and very mad'. Lord Kames, never one to take fools lightly, was tolerantly disposed, Adam Smith, as we have seen, had some time and regard for him. So, wearing his sober face, the young James was able to become a member of the Select Society, Edinburgh's leading debating club and a vital force in the Scottish Enlightenment. He was also (somewhat more surprising perhaps) elected a Mason – again ritual and mystery. But at this stage of his development, it is more realistic to picture Boswell in his element with other young bucks of the town, carousing, joking, sometimes whoring. He was a leading light in the Soapers' Club which met in a West Bow tavern on Tuesdays. There each man could 'soap his own beard' – do his own thing, in modern parlance – and jest and jape, without fear of offence or censure. To those who have enjoyed the warmth and conviviality of friends and colleagues in a High Street howf, with the bluster of an Edinburgh winter outside, the picture is a timeless one.

Boswell's poetry and pamphleteering have been characterised as bad verse and worse. True, much of it is boring, self-adulatory and of little lasting value. The *Beggar's Opera* and *Tristram Shandy* were all the rage. Much of his output apes the tone of such productions. But, amid the literary dross of these earlier years, there are little gems and nuggets that any twenty-one-year-old author could be proud of. Boswell could write and was beginning to realise it.

First (and foremost) on himself:

A Song:

B . . [oswell] of Soapers the King,
On Tuesdays at Thom's does appear,
And when he does talk or does sing
To him ne'er a one can come near,
For he talks with such ease and such grace,
That all charm'd to attention we sit
And he sings with so comic a face
That our sides are just ready to split.

He has all the bright fancy of youth,
With the judgement of forty and five;
In short, to declare the plain truth,
There is no better fellow alive!

And again (in a letter to Andrew Erskine, December 1761):

The author of the 'Ode to Tragedy' is a most excellent man... he has
a good, manly countenance, and he owns himself to be amourous;
he has infinite vivacity, yet is observed at times to have a melancholy
cast, he is rather fat than lean, rather short than tall, rather young
than old; his shoes are neatly made, and he never wears spectacles.
The length of his walking stick is not as yet ascertained, but we hope
soon to favour the republic of letters with the solution of this
difficulty, as several able mathematicians are employed in its
investigation, and for that purpose have posted themselves at
different given points in the Canongate; so that when the gentleman
saunters down to the Abbey of Holyrood House, in order to think of
ancient days, on King James V and Queen Mary, they may compute
his altitude above the street according to the rules of geometry.

All this would be quite insufferable if there were not abundant
independent evidence that he could indeed be a pleasant and gay
companion. In a letter addressed to Boswell while on his European travels
(1 July 1765), a long-term friend, George Dempster, chides Boswell for
being pompous and recalls:

Whatever alteration your ideas may have undergone, mine are still
the same. I still fancy myself admitted by Terry's maid, clambering

up two pair of stairs, sitting on a rush chair drinking tea out of a tin kettle; I figure you in your greasy nightcap taking physic, or perhaps strutting in plain pompadour like an officer of the Horse Guards, or perhaps just returned with a week's provisions from the chandler's shop, or lampooning Michael Ramsay, or begging Franks for Johnston or James Bruce, or waltering [rolling about] in my floor with Fingal or – or – or, blanks to be filled with circumstances ten times more ludicrous. If ever I hear a word more in your head upon the subject of dignity or decorum... Adieu, I will not sign my name, so farewell, you bitch.

For 'waltering' one could no doubt substitute rogering. And it appears that the term 'bitch' was a unisex term of abuse in the eighteenth century!

Then, on the subject of his friend Erskine's letters (25 August 1761):

Pray write to me soon. Your letters, I prophesy, will entertain me not a little; and will, besides, be extremely serviceable in many important respects; they will supply me with oil to my lamps, grease to my wheels, and blacking to my shoes. They will furnish me with strings to my fiddle, lashes to my whip, lining to my breeches, and buttons to my coat. They will make charming spurs, excellent knee-buckles, and inimitable watch-keys. In short, while they last, I shall neither want breakfast, dinner nor supper.

More seriously, in a letter to Johnston, 27 October 1762:

My Dear Friend:

A note will revive your spirits to see from whence this Epistle is dated, even from a place in which the happiest moments of your life have passed. While the multitude consider it just as the town of Edinburgh and no more; how much more valuable it is to you, who look upon it as an ancient city – the capital of Scotland... You also think of the Royal Palace of Holyrood House, the venerable church, the lofty mountain Arthurseat, the romantic Salisbury Craigs and the extensive Kings Park where you and I have had so many walks of pleasing meditation.

The same letter contains a reference to the twin passions of the young men at the time: the theatre and the English Church. But Boswell clearly had a feeling for Edinburgh and for its place in history – and this many years before Scott's historical novels made the romance of history the vogue. In an earlier letter to Johnston (13 September 1762):

> *I have read Robertson's History for the first time, which has carried me back in imagination to the ancient days of Scottish Grandeur; has filled my mind with generous ideas of the valour of our Ancestors, and made me feel a pleasing sympathy for the beautiful accomplished Mary... your mind will be filled... with curious ideas of France – churches lighted with wax candles – gilded prayer books – Prince Charles with a white feather in his hat – Old Jacobite Ladies drinking tea in a old carved room down a North closs, in the month of January – the Duke of Perth's family – a coach and six – an apartment with a large fire on – with a yellow damask bed and window curtains – fine carpet – splendid looking glasses – soft chairs etc. Oh Johnston, Johnston! what a lively fertile imagination I have. Are you not greatly diverted?*

Finally, on women:

> *B . . [oswell] does women adore,*
> *And never once means to deceive,*
> *He's in love with at least half a score –*
> *If they're serious he smiles in his sleeve...*

He could also write much more directly and crudely about his affairs with women; one thinks of the lively description of his night with Louisa in the *London Journal,* or of a letter of about this time when he boasts of a vigorous night with 'a strong-backed whore'.

Meantime, in the pursuit of women, Boswell had been active on several fronts. Mrs Cowper, the actress, had been supplanted by the more compliant Mrs Love. It will be recalled that she was the wife of his old actor-mentor. She was probably middle-aged herself and Boswell would sometimes jocularly refer to her as 'Old Canongate'. In the course of 1762, he fathered a child on one Peggy Doig and had to pay a fine to the Canongate Kirk Session. At the same time, he appears to have been conducting a more dangerous liaison with Jean, the seventeen-year-old married daughter of Lord Kames. This last was potential dynamite. Kames was a senior member of the judiciary, respected both as judge and philosopher. He and his wife had been kind and hospitable to Boswell. Adultery in the law of Scotland was still technically a crime. Adultery with the recently married young wife of a land-owning equal was a serious business indeed. More on Jean and James follows.

His private diaries of the period are laced with 'Tea: paradise'; 'In the forenoon had been with – ; one, she two, and visited A – '. And not content with all this, the bold James flirted with other marriageable young girls and even considered (briefly) an alliance with the recently widowed Duchess of Douglas, probably forty years his senior: }. . . if it succeeds, bravo! independence…'

So much, then, for reform and resolution. By March 1762, Lord Auchinleck had had enough. Despite the transmission of the estate being irrevocably restricted by an entail, so that it could only pass to his direct male heir (i.e. James), Lord Auchinleck nonetheless insisted that the young man sign a deed which purported to give the father power to transmit the management of the estate to trustees on his death, leaving the son only a portion of the estate income. In fact this did not happen, and it may have been a tactic on the part of the father to demonstrate to his son just how short his patience was becoming. As a sop, James was given a fixed income of £100 a year. Perhaps this development did bring Boswell to his senses. A bargain was struck with his father: he would apply himself and satisfy the Faculty entrance requirements. In return, his father agreed that he would be allowed to go south once more to seek a commission. So, for a time, all was industry again. And at the end of July 1762, Boswell did indeed pass the major Faculty exam in civil law. The scene was set for further and wider adventures.

But it was still the summertime. The London season did not start until Parliament reconvened later in the autumn. There was time for what Boswell called his 'Harvest Jaunt'.

CHAPTER 4

The Harvest Jaunt:
September – October
1762

Boswell's journal of this short trip through the south-west of
Scotland and the Border counties, is of importance in various
respects. It is the first full Boswell journal that we have. It
demonstrates the young man polishing up his considerable
literary talent for greater things. He wrote to Johnston, on 13 September
1762: 'I intend to keep a journal in order to acquire a method for doing it
when I launch into the Ocean of High Life.' It presents a unique and
personal picture of Scottish country life in the 1760s. But, most important
of all, it demonstrates Boswell's progress from being a writer of merely
ordinary competence, to one who was able to observe and record people,
situations and moods in a uniquely effective way, so as to present a living
picture. Through Boswell's journals, we are admitted into the past; to
experience through, and with him, the atmosphere of the times.

The journal of the jaunt is concerned very largely with Scotland and
Scots folk. Boswell was preparing himself to set sail on a larger sea. But for
the purpose of this book, it is valuable to have this Scottish journal to
savour. For this reason, and the more practical one that the material in the
journal is presently hard to come by, we should spend some time with the
twenty-one-year-old James as he rides on his autumn journey into the
country.

Boswell set off on his journey south 'about 8 o'clock' on the morning of
Tuesday, 14 September 1762. For the first leg of his trip, he had the
company of a friend, James Chalmers, and a servant lad, Walter Urie. The
travellers were in good spirits. They breakfasted a few miles south of

The Galloway Hills from Merrick.

Auchinleck, at the farmstead of Polquhairn and then headed up into the wild Ayrshire hills. At one point, Boswell's mare got stuck in the mud: 'while I threw myself off and lay extended on the rushy green with my *os sublime* levelled against the sky.'

As they jogged along the wild moor for the eight miles to Dalmellington, the travellers swapped stories to entertain each other. The first stop later in the day was at Barbeth, south of Dalmellington, where they were entertained to their main afternoon meal. Their hosts were hospitable but bucolic. After exhausting his 'little stock of country conversation', Boswell found himself 'heartily wearied' and anxious to be on his way. So too was his companion, 'upon whom the Laird had played several coarse jokes'. Thus, despite it being a very wet afternoon and their next destination being eight miles on through wild country, they took once more to horse.

The countryside between Dalmellington and Carsphairn is wild and hilly with occasional spectacular views of Loch Doon. The trio 'were severely pelted by a smart shower', but rode on 'with amazing celerity', invigorated by the exercise and the prospect of better company ahead. Good training for the Guards, thought Boswell.

We came into Lagwine as it grew dark, and found it a most hospitable retreat. Never did I look upon an apartment with so much satisfaction as upon the parlour there, neatly boxed round and papered on the roof, with a handsome carpet on the floor; a large fire blazing in the chimney and two young ladies at needlework with contentment in their looks… Everything at supper was neat and clean, and after the cloth was removed we had a bottle of genuine Madeira brought home by Captain McAdam. Miss McAdam is a fine sensible, good humoured lively girl, and sings prettily. We played parts of The Beggar's Opera, I Macheath, and she Polly, really very well, and whenever the song was done, Fingland gave unfeigned applause. I was here perfectly happy.

Boswell and his companion spent the next day very agreeably at the McAdams. The household had a great number of children; one, then six, was the John McAdam whose future road-building prowess was to revolutionise roads in Scotland and elsewhere. Boswell, not quite twenty-two himself, romped with the children and staged a macabre game of 'Courts' for their amusement and terror. 'I contrived it so that they should be guilty of what I termed enormous crimes, for which they were to be ordered for immediate execution and made the one with the most curious visage the macer, and had sentences pronounced against the felons in the rhodomontade style of our Courts of Justice, and then, with their hands

The gaunt ruins of Kenmure Castle as they stand today.

behind their backs, made a fashion of whipping them through the town, an operation with which they were highly delighted.' Already, it seems, Boswell's reluctant fascination with his ultimate profession was beginning to oust the Guards.

The next day, the small party rode on southwards towards New Galloway, to Kenmure Castle. As one comes out of the Ayrshire hills into the Stewartry of Kirkcudbright, the country softens and becomes green and picturesque. Boswell describes Kenmure as 'a very noble place. The house is situated on a beautiful hill (like Hardyknute's); behind it are wild mountains and woods; before it a pretty plain with the river of Ken running into a lake seven miles in length, of which you have a large stretch under your eyes finely diversified with natural islands.' Kenmure still stands, now a vast and picturesque ruin on its mound. Boswell goes on to sketch his host and hostess:

> *My Lord received me in the kindest manner. He is a man of good heart, a cheerful temper, and uncommon genius. He has seen much of the world, knows mankind well, and reads a great deal. As his fortune is not great and as he married Lord Seaforth's sister, he retired to the country, where he makes life very agreeable. He is fond of all country sports; he reads, and he now and then has company. He tells a story with much life and sings a comical song extremely well. As he has not many neighbours, he contrives to make the most of all the two legged animals near him, and in a manner creates companions... We were introduced to my Lady, who is prodigiously handsome and is still a very fine woman. She was in France from 4 year old to 18, and has a deal of vivacity and politeness, and looks much like a woman of fashion.*

Even when full of life, there may have been something forbidding about the old castle.

> *Friday 17th September: I had been somewhat gloomy during the night. I slept in a large bed chamber in a wing of the house detached from the rest. The drawing room was next door to me, in which hung a portrait of the Lord Kenmure who was executed for high treason upon Tower Hill in the year 1716. As the terror for ghosts was strongly impressed upon my imagination when young – although I have now got the better of it, yet it will now and then*

recur upon me – I began to imagine that the beheaded Viscount
would be that night sent to me to reveal something of importance
with respect to the family. However, I awaked this morning, serene
and well, and came to breakfast in a most charming humour.

Lady Kenmure, in any event, had no trouble in sensing how to deal with
the young Boswell. She flirted with him:

my Lady and I were as fond as you can imagine… At tea my Lady
was uncommonly lively, sung little pretty chansons, tripped lightly
through the room, wrapped her capuchin round me and lisped such
little expressions of tenderness as are used to children of whom one is
fond… Her behaviour was such to me that, had she been an
Englishwoman, I should have concluded that I had her affections
and that an intrigue would not be displeasing. But as I looked upon
her Ladyship as une dame de France, I was perfectly convinced that
it was only the overflowing of a gaieté de coeur, and especially as my
Lord was present, I considered all her little douceurs as the sportive
expressions of innocent gallantry. At the same time I could not help
being elated with the liking which she so obviously showed for me.

Boswell had fun with his host as well. Among Lord Kenmure's scarce
companions was one Nathan McKie, whom Boswell describes as 'a strong
Caliban of a clergyman'. Apparently the minister and His Lordship amused
themselves by addressing verses to each other. There is extant a challenge
and reply in verse to a curling match. Because of this friendly rivalry, Lord
Kenmure had composed a piece of doggerel which he called *'Nathan's
Complaint'*. The gist of it is as follows:

Alas, what a brute I have been,
My talents thus to misapply,
On curling and rhyming so keen;
Some other vocation I'll try.

A shit-house I'll build with my stones,
As they in my Parish are scarce;
And with dull poems, ohone!
I'll use them in wiping my a- !

As we know, the young Boswell himself was not above bad verse and, in a collection of poems from a volume in the Bodleian Library (published in 1974 as *Boswell's Book of Bad Verse*, edited by Jack Werner), there is a 'Song to Lord Kenmure':

> *To render you bright with choicest liquor at night*
> *Take punch made of rum that is double,*
> *And I give you this charge, be your bowl full and large*
> *To content the good Laird of Craigubble.*

> *In this world there are few, that are sound men and true,*
> *Or who will for their neighbours take trouble,*
> *But to Kirroughtree a safe pilot to me*
> *Has been the good Laird of Craigubble.*

How His Lordship felt about being styled the Laird of Craigubble is not recorded!

On the Saturday, Boswell left the hospitable laird 'with much cordiality', and set off south-west over the hills towards Kirroughtree, near Newton Stewart. This is a wild, moorland road, more like the Highlands than the south of Scotland. 'We... rode 12 miles upon a hard stoney road, encompassed with high mountains, mostly barren and rocky. We got to Kirrochtree about 3 o'clock and had a very kind reception from Mr and Mrs Heron and Lady Kames.'

The visit to Kirroughtree was, in fact, the principal purpose for the 'Jaunt'. As earlier hinted, it seems probable that Boswell was having an adulterous affair with the young Jean Heron. Seventeen years of age at the time, and recently married to Patrick Heron, the Laird of Kirrochtree, she was the daughter of Lord and Lady Kames. She appears to have been spirited and good-looking. Given her social standing and the Scottish *mores* of the time, she must also have been reckless and foolhardy. The evidence in favour of the liaison is surveyed by Professor Pottle in the *Earlier Years*. He concludes that Jean is very likely to have been the 'daughter of the man of the first distinction in Scotland' who 'married a gentleman of great wealth' and who 'let me see that she loved me more than she did her husband. She made no difficulty of granting me all.' This from the *Sketch of My Life* which Boswell wrote two years later, to introduce himself to Rousseau.

If further proof be needed, it can be found in another of the poems from the collection quoted, which the lovelorn James appears to have written to Jean, very possibly on this occasion. Entitled 'An Epistle to Miss Home', the essence of it is as follows:

Demure as witch's tabby cat
Have I, th' illustrious Boswell, sat
I'm sure at least for minutes five
Beating my skull how to contrive
A few sweet, pretty lines to write
To your sweet, pretty self, tonight.

Lord Kames shall stupid be, and rude,
Nor labour for the public good;
My lady strut in haughty state
And mirth and easy humour hate;
And George [Jean's brother] become with head agog
An overbearing, blust'ring dog –
E'er you, my Jeanie, in this heart
Have not at least a little part
In way of friendship or of love
God rest my dear, my name's above.

Nor would you coldly, prudish blame
My French romantic, am'rous flame,
But with a soft complacence say:
'I let the Soaper have his way'.
Think you I ever shall forget
Your goodness – will you take a bet?
I would advise you not to lay,
Unless you have a mind to pay.

All in all, one of the young man's better efforts in verse: a tender, loving poem.

So far as the journal was concerned however, the sentiment could not be too openly expressed. Boswell intended the account of his jaunt to be read by his friends Johnston and McQhae, who, presumably, were not privy to this dangerous romance. Thus he had to content himself by describing his lover as:

Mrs Heron, though not what one would style a flaming beauty, is a very elegant woman. Her person is tall and genteel, and her face is very lovely and expressive of good sense and sweetness of disposition… She has an excellent understanding and has had a complete education in every respect. She has a great deal of vivacity and an inimitable vein of drollery. Her sallies of humour, however, are always chastised by a delicate correctness of behaviour, which she possesses in a high degree, and which she owes to the affectionate care of her worthy parents. She esteems and loves her husband, equally free from an affected coldness on one hand and a foolish fondness on the other. She promises to make a good wife, and a very complete woman; to be a comfort and ornament to her friends, and to show a bright example of the influence of a rational and polite plan of education. Mr Heron is sensible, genteel, well-bred, has an uncommon good temper, and, at the same time, has all the spirit that becomes a man.

This is doubly ironic. First, there is the passing mention of his host. Second, the styling of his own lover as the incipient 'good wife'. In fact, Jean eventually went too far. Ten years later, in January 1772, Patrick Heron divorced her on the ground of her adultery with a young Ensign and she was dispatched in disgrace and exile to Paris by her grieving father. Many years later (*Journal,* 29 November 1782), Boswell had a first-hand account of the disgrace and the dispatch from Lady Kames. At that time Jean was still in France, existing on an allowance of £80 annually from her father, plus £10 and 'some linens' from her mother. One would dearly like to know what eventually became of the strong-willed, profligate Jean. Throughout this long conversation with her mother Boswell, the perfect hypocrite, kept himself 'steady', amazed at his own 'vigour of mind'. And mightily relieved too, no doubt.

In fact, Boswell stayed on at Kirroughtree, or in the neighbourhood, for over a fortnight. He busied himself with his journal. He started a collection of 'good stories and bon mots', which he styled 'Boswelliana'. He read much, sometimes aloud to the others. On the night of Tuesday, 21 September, he notes that he read Swift's 'Letter to a Young lady Newly Married', and some papers of the *Rambler* to the company. The author of the latter was, of course, Dr Johnson, the future subject of *The Life*. 'I cannot help differing from… my learned friends, with regard to the author of the *Rambler*. They will allow him nothing but heaviness, weakness and affected pedantry. Whereas, in my opinion, Mr Johnson is a man of much philosophy, extensive reading, and real knowledge of human life.' Thus, eight months before his momentous encounter with the great man himself, Boswell was already taking the part of his future hero.

Wednesday brought a comic episode.

At seven in the morning, Mr Heron proposed that we should go a-hunting. This exercise I was pretty much a stranger to, and was not well equipped for, having two horses which I bought for thirteen pounds. However, I mounted my six pounder and away we went to the field, where we soon had a very good chase, which I kept tolerably up at; only could not bring myself to venture a leap which now and then threw me out for a little. After this was over, I felt myself so fond of it that I insisted upon having another, which very soon presented itself. But alas, while I, elated with an immediate view, galloped on fearless and unconcerned, my mare gave a sudden spring and I found her plunging in a deep broad ditch, the sides of which were almost choked up with ferns. I threw myself to the opposite side, but was up to the haunches in water, in which, however, I did not long continue. The bottom of the ditch being a thick mud, and the sides a good deal raised above the surface of the water, it was very difficult to get out again, and I stood like a statue of anxiety wrought by the hand of a Phidias, under much apprehension that she might be drowned and I deprived the half of my cavalry. However, by the seasonable aid of one of Heron's servants, John Cowie, a judicious active fellow, we had her fairly relieved without her sustaining any damage. I then got upon a spirited hunter of Heron's. But finding her very headstrong and skittish, and being convinced that, while I was afraid, I could not relish the sport, I quitted her for my seven pounder, and thus could boast that I had changed three horses; although like a man who has changed many wives, I perhaps lost as much as I gained. I now rode secure and had a noble chase.

Lord and Lady Kames were fellow guests at Kirroughtree. At this time, Henry Home, Lord Kames, friend and patron of David Hume and Adam Smith, was sixty-six, and at the height of his powers as lawyer and philosopher. He had been counsel to the unfortunate Captain Porteous in 1736; in 1741 he had published his great *Dictionary of Decisions*, the first

Henry Home, Lord Kames (1696 - 1782), philosopher, jurist and friend to the young Boswell.

comprehensive digest of the judgments of the Scottish courts. In the very year in which Boswell was writing, his famous *Elements of Criticism* had appeared. He had been a judge of the Court of Session since 1752 and was to sit on for a further twenty years until his death at the age of eighty-six. In his valuable chapter on Kames in *The Scottish Jurists* (1985), Professor D. M. Walker describes him as: 'a leading figure in the Scottish Enlightenment, he was a jurist and judge, author and literary critic, philosopher and improving landlord.'

Boswell gives this sketch of him in his journal:

> *Lord Kames is a man of uncommon genius, great application, an extensive knowledge, of which his various works are a standing proof. It is indeed astonishing to find a man so much master of law, philosophy, and the belles lettres, and possessed of so great insight into human nature, and at the same time a good companion, cheerful and lively. Although he is now and then a little whimsical and impatient with contradiction, he is honest, friendly and public spirited, and is upon the whole a great character.*

Kirroughtree today: a comfortable hotel now occupies the site of
the Heron family home.

At a later stage, Boswell had it in mind to write Kames's biography. Kames
was agreeable, as long as it was flattering! Although materials were
gathered, the project came to nothing and it was left to a colleague, Lord
Woodhouselee, to write the first detailed account of the great man, in 1814.
Jean was not mentioned.

Boswell was also anxious to cultivate Lady Kames. He describes her thus:

Lady Kames was very handsome and still has a very good presence.
She is a woman of good understanding and very well bred. Regulates
her family with accuracy, and has in her house and at her table a
remarkable degree of elegance. She has a great fund of humour, and
a peculiar turn of strong and brilliant propriety of expression. She
has now and then a little lowness of spirits, which renders her more
apt to be stirred and offended than one would wish, and makes her
say pretty severe things. But take her all in all, she is an excellent
woman.

Boswell was to remain on intimate terms with both of them throughout the
remainder of their lives. He was with Lord Kames within a few hours of his
death.

But that was twenty years ahead. At Kirroughtree, Lady Kames was already in residence and Lord Kames arrived on 22 September, 'which gave universal joy'. On the 23rd: 'In the forenoon we walked out to show Lord Kames the place. It is a pretty good mixture, having behind it wild hills, and before it a pretty plain with the bay of Wigtown. In the hollow about a mile to the South runs the river of Cree, upon which stand the villages of Minnigaff and Newton Stewart. Mr Heron has a good house and gardens and a good many trees.'

Another guest, Murray of Broughton, the Laird of Gatehouse of Fleet, was consulted as to the Guards. 'He told me very obligingly, "Sir, I can do little for you. But I shall gladly run about."' Boswell's hopes of an (elegant) army career were still high.

On the 25th, Boswell left Kirroughtree for a time to be a guest of the Earl of Galloway at Galloway House. This would be a pleasant ride of sixteen miles or so, along the side of Wigtown Bay to the vast red sandstone pile which still stands there in its park. Boswell noted: 'It is well situated, being enclosed on three sides by the sea, which is a thing very seldom to be found. The house was designed by John Douglas, a blockhead of an architect. It is very heavy and very ill laid out.' At night, the family went to cards. Boswell got the key of the library, 'which contains a very good collection in very good order and, I imagine, not much hurt by being used'. The next day he mentioned, 'I did not find myself happy here. I was under restraint and my genius was cramped. Their table, though plentiful, was yet narrow, and you seemed to be fed by measure. I had a cold damp room, and in short I like to think of quitting it next day.' He may have been missing Jean, because he added: 'I felt a sensation upon my getting to Kirrochtrie like what one feels upon getting home.'

There was another side trip to Wigtown, where Lord Auchinleck had formerly been Sheriff. Boswell describes the place as being 'very well situated, and as it has a very broad street and many good houses, it is really a pretty village, or rather town, for I should be sorry to give it an appellation anyhow inferior to what it deserves'. Boswell's description could still be applied: Wigtown today seems like a small town which time has passed by. Two later additions now dominate the town: a disproportionately large town hall and a monument on the hill above, to the Covenanter martyrs of the 1680s, who were drowned for their faith. Boswell was welcomed by the good townspeople: 'Ay, ay, he's just like his worthy father.' While Boswell was there the council elected Lord

Springkell House, Kirkconnel: the handsome mansion dating from the 1740s.

Auchinleck to be their Lord Provost. Given the distance of Auchinleck (about forty-five miles) and his judicial duties, the appointment must have been a purely honorary one.

The visit to Kirroughtree was now almost over. After a few days more of socialising, Boswell noted on Sunday, 3 October:

And now I am come to my last evening at Kirrochtrie. Mr Samuel Johnson says that there are few things of which one can say without regret: 'This is the last'. How much more must that be the case when we are going to leave what is particularly agreeable to us. Such was my situation this night, when I had the prospect of leaving next day, my dear Mrs Heron, of whom, were I to express all my feelings, I should certainly fall under the censure of an overheated imagination. She was very good and sympathised with me, with much tenderness, which was extraordinary, as people generally laugh at distress of that kind. But that is owing to a want of sensibility, of which this sweet creature has a very great share. Monday 4th October. On a fine frosty morning, not too cold, we left Kirroughtree Mrs Heron and I had some serious conversation before I parted with her, not to meet again in all probability for a very long time.

Boswell's travels to London and the Continent started later that year and he was not to return until 1766. It is not recorded whether he met Jean again, prior to her disgrace in 1772. If he did, it was no longer as her lover. Ironically, her ex-husband, Patrick Heron, was to marry Boswell's cousin, Lady Betty Cochrane, in 1775 and Boswell was frequently in his company thereafter.

With Kirroughtree behind, the pace of Boswell's jaunt quickened. Now in company with Lord and Lady Kames, he travelled eastwards through the green Kirkcudbright countryside, dining at Gatehouse and with stops at Gelston, near Castle Douglas, and at the George Inn, Dumfries. Boswell's next significant port of call was to be at Springkell, near Ecclefechan.

Springkell House, dating from the 1740's, still sits very handsomely in picturesque grounds. For long a seat of the Maxwell family, the incumbent laird at the time of Boswell's visit was Sir William, a distant cousin. Boswell describes the household thus:

Sir William Maxwell is a man of a handsome figure and genteel air, and carries in his external appearance the character which is much talked about and seldom found, a gentleman. He has a great deal of good sense, sweetness of disposition, and a delicacy of taste. He is perfectly easy and polite and may be styled, in every sense of the word, a pretty man. Miss Maxwell, his sister, is an honest-hearted merry, jocular girl, of size somewhat corpulent but has a very agreeable countenance and can walk and dance with all imaginable cleverness. She plays with taste upon the guitar, which she chiefly employs in accompanying her voice with a thorough-bass… Her voice is clear, strong and sweet. She has great command of it and sings with uncommon spirit and taste. She obliged us with several Italian airs and English ballads. She likewise gave us 'Galashiels', 'I'll Never Leave Thee', 'O the Broom', and some others of the best Scotch songs, in which she expressed more tenderness of feeling than I ever heard.

On Friday, 8 October:

Sir William and I walked about the place, which as Lord Chalkstone says, has great capabilities. There is a fine walk for near two miles upon the side of the river, and a pretty variety of grounds about his house, which is a very good one. Sir William has a turn for improving, and will probably make Springkell much better. He has here a good many old trees, particularly about the old churchyard of Kirkconnel, which Parish is now joined with another. There are here a great many tombstones as also the family burial place, with a little chapel above the vault. The place has a pleasing melancholy about it and is admirably suited for calm meditation.

One of the pleasing things about the Scottish countryside is its unchanging nature. it is still possible to follow Boswell's footsteps over the fields, by the river, to the old chapel, now ruined, and to reflect with him on the legend of Helen of Kirkconnel.

A tradition goes that there lived a pretty woman of the name of Helen here who had two lovers, one of whom discovered her one day walking with his rival and immediately levelled his gun at him, which Helen perceived, ran in between them to save him, but from the same shot they both received death. The unfortunate lover went abroad to relieve his mind from the thought, where he composed a mournful ditty:

> *I wish I were where Helen lies*
> *In fair Kirkconnel lea.*

The old churchyard Kirkconnell.

Brampton, Cumbria, Howard Arms Lane: part of the old coaching Inn.

The fact that Boswell is recounting this as an existing tradition rather belies the cautionary notice in the chapel grounds that the tale may be just an eighteenth century invention.

Boswell and his party spent about a week in the pleasant surrounds of Springkell. Saturday, 9 October: 'Walking, music, chatting and indolent lolling, employed the forenoon.' Monday, 1 October:

We walked about all the forenoon in that sort of agreeable
sauntering way which, when the sun shines and the weather is
gentle, disposes much to serenity and good humoured disposition. In
the afternoon arrived from Carlisle… Dr Coultard, an apothecary, a
true-looking Englishman with a round-cut head and leather
breeches, a jolly dog who sang us the song that the boy sings who
sweeps Drury-Lane stage before the candles are lighted, to the tune of
'Balance a straw':

Though I sweep to and fro, yet I'd have you to know
There are sweepers in high life as well as in low

Again, a well-turned cameo of the good doctor.

Another visitor was a Miss Kitty Gilpin, 'a fine lively creature, not pretty but of an agreeable countenance… After dinner… I discovered that Miss Gilpin was an excellent mimic. So I made fair exchange with her, and gave her Logan and Lord Dundonald and Sir George Preston and Lord Dumfries, for as many of her acquaintances. I contrived to make our personages talk together, which was a most ludicrous scene… the company… were quite distressed with laughing.' (Unfortunately, word of the 'ludicrous scene' eventually came to Lord Auchinleck's ear. He was also 'distressed', as James was to learn).

On Wednesday, 13 October, the party left Springkell and travelled south, via Longtown, to Brampton. The intention was to travel east towards Kames in Berwickshire, since 'the road through England… is much better and takes us but a day longer to travel than the road by Edinburgh would have done.' What seems like quite a deviation to the modern traveller was then dictated by the poor communications of the time.

Boswell's journal comes sparkling to life in the passage about his stay in Brampton. He describes the place as 'a very good little village, prettily situated'. It is now, of course, a stirring market town with a population of about 4,000.

It still has its market square and its old inns. When Boswell arrived, the place was in a stir:

When we entered the village, we were met by a crowd huzzaing a man who was beating a drum for a puppet show, and had, moreover, another man with him who carried, high elevated on a lofty pole, a hat and four halfpenny cakes. This last circumstance puzzled me a good deal; but I learnt that as many boys were to eat the loaves, and he who was first done eating was to have the hat. We had here an excellent inn. I was happy and cheerful; and I resolved to see the show, which raised my curiosity as I had never seen Punch, which indeed is unaccountable. Accordingly, at seven, to the Town's Hall, where the exhibition was to be, full of vivacity and that kind of feeling which we carry to the theatre when we expect to see a diverting play. The room was pretty well filled with a very curious collection of human beings. An impudent dog sat by me who wanted much to cultivate an acquaintance with me; but I repudiated him. Next to him sat a jolly gentleman in black, whose name was Dean. As I had my Bath great-coat with a gold binding, my gold laced hat smartly set upon my head, and twirled my cane switch with a good deal of gentility, I looked exceedingly like an officer of the Army. My Dean therefore showed me respect; 'Come, Captain, take a snuff,' which I received with a hearty nod and a 'Thank you, Mr Dean.' We bought apples and carried them about in our hats to the company with inimitable civility and address, and so were very principal people.

Boswell then goes on to describe the performance itself, but it is clear that, in his eye at least, he was the principal performer. He continues:

Little did I think when I entered this scene of rude amusement that the gentle Goddess of Love was laying snares for me. However, that was the case. On the bench behind me sat a young lady in a red cloak and black hat, very like, but younger and handsomer, than Lady Dunmore. I instantly addressed myself to her in the most engaging manner that I could, found her tender enough; and during the hubbub, I obtained from her the sweetest kiss that virgin ever gave. She told me that she was maid to an innkeeper in the town, and that she could not have an opportunity of seeing me. However, she agreed that she would go to London with me if I would take her. Dear little creature! How fond was I of her. Punch and the other puppets next appeared, who diverted me much, but my girl went to another seat and when I followed her, was excessively prudish. Whether she observed some acquaintance that she stood in awe of, or for what other reason, I could not imagine; but while my mind was occupied with mingled concern and merriment, I was sent for by my fellow travellers, to supper and was obliged to leave my charmer…

At supper I fell much in love with the chamber-maid who served us, who was a handsome girl with an insinuating wantonness of look. I made her light me to my room, and when I had her there, she indulged me in many endearments, but would by no means consent to the main object of my ardent desires, and seemed afraid of the people of the house hearing us make noise. So I was obliged to sleep by myself. However, I discovered that sleep prevented me from felicity, for Lord Kames' servant joked me next morning and told me seriously that he had saw her go into my room and shut the door after I was gone to bed. This was going pretty far; but I suppose she had not assurance enough to wake me.

Hadrian's Wall, as it runs across the wild Northumberland countryside.

Either that, or the servant was pulling the young soaper's leg!

The passage quoted is a wonderfully lively one, and looks forward to Boswell's method of recording people, places and events, perfected in the *London Journal*.

After the excitement of Brampton, the party had a long journey to the east before reaching their destination in Berwickshire. The road taken was the old high road that runs, cheek by jowl with Hadrian's Wall, along the vast, bleak escarpment of the Northumberland Hills. Boswell does not mention the wall, which is surprising as it must have been a feature of the journey. It may just have been that the party was on the road and intent on making progress.

The days were long ones. They passed by Chollerton (which Boswell refers to as 'Collerford'):

> *where there was a numerous meeting of gentlemen of Northumberland; well-dressed people, plump and vivacious. We went at night to Cambo, a village very small and very poor. The inn was indeed exceedingly bad. When we entered we first beheld a company in the parlour mortally drunk. We were shown into the only other room, which was raw and confused. The landlady was a shrew and the maids were slovenly and dirty. Everything was worse than the*

Kames, near Coldstream, the old house described by Boswell.

*worst inn in Scotland. I now felt the disadvantage of too much
delicacy of taste. I was shocked and really put out of humour and
expressed my uneasiness and rage very strongly. Lady Kames
grumbled a little but my Lord said not a word. He thought it was
below a philosopher to be affected by such trivial inconveniences... I
had a bed in the parlour, which I had a great aversion at; I kept on
all my clothes except my coat and boots, and made the best of it.*

Perhaps by way of retribution, Boswell left messages inscribed on the
windows of the inn, purporting to be signed by Tobias Smollett, David
Hume and Lord Kames. Even his graffiti had to be of the best!

On the Saturday afternoon (16 October), the party at last reached
Kames, a little to the north of Coldstream. Boswell himself gives 'a little
sketch of the place: The house is old and not very good, but the most is
made of every bit of space in it, and the rooms are neatly fitted up. There
is a pretty lawn before the house, with trees scattered up and down. There
is a group of good enclosures, a handsome garden, and before the house a
long gravel walk and banks ornamented with flowers and evergreens.'
Boswell was to be a guest of Lord and Lady Kames for ten days. He was
obviously pleased to be so far on his way. He notes: 'We were very hearty
this night, and I rejoiced much finding myself lodged in a sweet handsome
bedroom.'

But, in truth, the visit was not a success. As we have noted, Boswell's temperament was mercurial. He could sparkle one day and be in the depths of low spirits the next. Unfortunately, it was the turn of depression. Monday, 18 October: 'I was very dull this day. I despise myself. I was silent and made no kind of show.' Thursday, 19 October: 'The day turned bad. I was still out of spirits. I walked up and down the room, I took up my German flute, played a little, was not pleased, laid it down again, tried to read, but had no attention, nor any relish for it. Attempted to write but could do nothing. Was glad when night came and I got to bed'.

On the Wednesday, there was to be horse-racing at Kelso. Although still feeling out of sorts, Boswell overcame an aversion to go:

At last a very prevailing motive occurred, which was the want of money; and I had a delicacy in asking it of Lord Kames, I resolved to go and search gold. When I came upon the turf, I felt a little vivacity at the sight of the equipages and horses, but that soon went off, and I rode up and down without any feeling, laughing at mankind for engaging in such ridiculous pursuits and despising the whole species – a most disagreeable situation of mind. I lost sixpence at a bet, which was all that I had, and thus I had not a single farthing. I applied to Lord Kellie who, as brother to Captain Erskine, and he was always fond of me, made my application the easier. With all imaginable gaiety I asked his Lordship to let me have five guineas, which he did most politely. I felt a strong regard for him and was pleased at the romantic conceit of getting it from a gamester, a nobleman, and a musical composer...”

for this was the famous Earl of Kellie.

However, low spirits prevailed. Boswell quarrelled with Lady Kames. Saturday, 22 October: 'She was somewhat sour. I imagined her more so, and thought she behaved to me as to one who was hanging on about the house. I had nothing to entertain my Lord with. I thought he was tired of me, I was tired of being here and vexed to find that the high opinion which we entertain of distinguished people flies off on being much with them. This is perhaps my fault and occasioned by my excessive love of novelty'. Perhaps Lady Kames had sensed that something had been going on between her daughter and Boswell. In any event, on a wet, windy morning (Thursday, 20 October), he took leave of Lord Kames, 'who seemed displeased somewhat' and took horse for Edinburgh.

I rode fourteen long computed miles through a wild country and deep roads – indeed the roads in the Merse are the worst that I ever saw; you just labour through a deep stiff clay, much more terrible than in Ayrshire – and when I came to Ginglekirk [Channelkirk] the public house was the only building and two wooden tents, one for a kitchen, another for a dining room, were the only places of entertainment. This was very uncomfortable. However, I stayed here an hour. I had then thirteen more of the long miles to Edinburgh. I got a boy going in upon an errand who was company to me in some measure. We stopped at Foord Bridge [Ford] and corned our horses and I treated him with small beer. The prospect of the Firth of Forth, the Lomond Hills, Arthur Seat, and the ancient city of Edina pleased me exceedingly. I wondered at the time how any external objects could make such an impression upon me.

In fact, Boswell does himself an injustice as to the distance he had covered. From Kames to Edinburgh is about forty-five miles. Boswell is obviously here talking about the old Scots mile of almost 2,000 yards. Even so, and in difficult conditions, he had travelled much more than the twenty-seven miles he computes.

Edinburgh in the late 18th century by Alexander Nasmyth.

Boswell's relief at being back in Edinburgh was quite palpable.

I got in about seven to Ferrier's at Bristo Port, where I put up my horse and bespoke a bed for myself. I went immediately and called upon Mrs Love, who is a smart, clever, good humoured creature, and a very lively actress. She was very glad to see me, and little Billy, her son, was quite overjoyed… I asked her to let me have a bed in her house, which after seeking about for, we found packed up in a hogshead for going to London, as she was to set out in a week or two. The incident was humorous enough and might make a good comic tale.

The incident of the bed is, of course, tongue in cheek, as Mrs Love was 'Old Canongate', the complaisant mistress.

So, once more back in the Edinburgh round. But even yet, the jaunt was not completely over. After a few days, on 30 October, Boswell put himself on a boat from Leith to Kinghorn, to visit his friend Andrew Erskine at Kellie in Fife and

when I arrived I was received with roars of applause, and kindness and exaltation. Captain Erskine is a tall black man with a great sagaciousness of countenance. He has an awkward bashfulness among strangers, but with his friends is easy and excellent company. He has a richness of imagination, a wildness of fancy, a strength of feeling, and a fluency of expression which render him a very fine poet. He has a great deal of humour and simplicity of manners. He has a turn for speculation and has none of the common notions of mankind.

As mentioned, Erskine and Boswell had been correspondents, sending facetious letters to one another, which they were later to publish. Erskine himself appears to have been prone to depression. In September 1793 he was to commit suicide by throwing himself into the Firth of Forth with his clothes weighed down by stones; an event which left Boswell 'affected with a kind of stupor, mixed with regret'. But these dreary events were years away. For the moment, all was good talk and good fun. Sunday, 31 October: 'multitudes of literary anecdotes'.

On 2 November the two friends returned together to Edinburgh. 'It was a pretty rough day, and I was pretty much afraid, but sung and joked all the way. We got to Leith in an hour. We went to Oman's, drank tea, and took a hackney-coach to town. Erskine and I were sat down at the Nether Bow and went immediately to the shop of Mr Alexander Donaldson, where we were much respected and entertained with literary news.'

The next day, Boswell and Erskine visited David Hume: 'We found him in his house in James's Court, in a good room newly fitted up, hung around with Strange's prints. He was sitting at his ease reading Homer.' Coincidentally, this is a description of a house Boswell was to stay in after his marriage. With Hume, the talk was all of the contemporary literary scene: Smollett, 'Ossian' Macpherson, Dr Johnson's pension and the 'Elements' of Lord Kames.

I asked Mr Hume to write more. He said he had done enough and was almost ashamed to see his own bulk on a shelf. We paid him a few compliments in pleasant mirth. Thus did an hour and a half of our existence move along. We were very happy. I showed a way, started subjects, and now and then spoke tolerably, much better than my knowledge entitles me to do. I have remembered the heads and the very words of a great part of Mr Hume's conversation with us. We left him and went to Mrs Loves…

But the days in Scotland were running out. Lord and Lady Auchinleck came to town and, having seen them, James decided to leave for London the following Monday, 15 November 1762. His father agreed to clear the young man's debts and to allow him £200 per year (approximately £20,000 in today's values). Boswell observed: 'This made me perfectly happy. It was all that I could ask.'

So, the preparations made, the jaunting over, and the serious travels about to start, at ten o'clock on the Monday morning, the twenty-two-year-old Boswell got into his chaise in the High Street of Old Edinburgh. Pausing only to take a last look at the Park and the Palace of Holyrood, he rattled off south to London and his European travels. He was not to see Scotland again for three and a half years.

CHAPTER 5

The Travelling Years:
London and Europe
1763 -1766

The three and a half years between November 1762 and March 1766, which Boswell spent in London and Europe, were crucial to the young man's development In that latter year he could write to Rousseau: 'I am no longer the sensitive, worried, self-doubting young man of the Val de Travers. I am a man'. And, in some ways, he had matured. In others, he never would. On any view, these years had been a marvellous success. He had met and formed a lifelong friendship with Dr Johnson. He had travelled with the veteran Earl Marischal, one of the most renowned Scotsmen of the times. He had met both Rousseau and Voltaire. And he was about to establish his literary fame with his *Account of Corsica,* published in 1768, based on his visit to the island towards the end of 1765. But our theme is Boswell the Scot, so an outline of the main events of his travels will suffice for our purpose.

A continuing concern was the young man's relationship with his father. We have seen how Lord Auchinleck had extreme reservations about what he conceived as James's flightier ideas. There were no shortage of these. At first the Guards were very much to the fore. Much of Boswell's activity in London after his arrival in November 1762 involved the search for a patron to help him to obtain a commission. There was also the search for a compliant mistress. By the Christmas of 1762 he had found the one, if not the other. He embarked on the brief, delicious and latterly disastrous affair with the actress, Louisa. This is vividly and amusingly described in the *London Journal,* written by Boswell in instalments and sent off to his friend John Johnston in Scotland. As to the other project, once it became

Wilkes & Liberty,
by Hogarth, 1763.

plain that the only commission likely to be available would be one in a 'marching regiment', the plan for a military life was abandoned in favour of a year's study in Holland and further travels thereafter.

The early 1760s were mixed times for a young Scot in London. Since the union of the Scottish and English parliaments in 1707, the focus of power in the government of Scotland had moved south to London. Those seeking places and patronage had necessarily to pay their court in the metropolis. For many years, Scottish affairs had been effectively managed by the Duke of Argyll through the local agency of Andrew Fletcher, Lord Milton. George II had died in 1760 and Argyll in 1761. The succession of George III meant the advancement of Argyll's nephew, Lord Bute, as Chief Minister. It was to Bute that Lord Kames directed his request for appointment as a Lord of Justiciary in April 1763. And it was to Bute that Lord Eglinton, on Boswell's behalf, made overtures for a commission in the Guards for him. The ascendancy of what was seen as a Scots faction was not at all popular in

Dr Samuel Johnson (1709 - 84) as he was in about 1777. Oil-sketch by James Barry.

certain political quarters. John Wilkes and his circle had been tormenting the government and Monarchy with an anti-establishment newspaper, the *North Briton*, the *Private Eye* of its day. Number 45 of this publication proved too strong for the government and King: Wilkes was arrested and imprisoned in the Tower of London. Boswell was in town during these stirring times (May 1763), but it was not the best moment for a relatively unconnected young Scot to make his overtures to those in power.

The time in London, of course, sets the scene for Boswell's famous meeting with Dr Johnson. The doctor was then a celebrated author and sage aged fifty-three. Boswell had been hoping and making opportunities for a meeting with the great man since his arrival in town. When the meeting did come, it came as a complete surprise. Boswell was taking tea in the back room of a bookshop belonging to one Thomas Davies. The date was 16 May 1763. Dr Johnson arrived unexpectedly and was ushered into the company. For once discountenanced and unprepared, Boswell was introduced by Davies as a young Scotsman. Boswell: 'I do indeed come from Scotland, but I cannot help it.' Johnson: 'That, sir, I find is what a very great many of your countrymen cannot help.' This typically brusque Johnsonian riposte was well deserved in the circumstances. Despite this bad start, the Boswell charm ultimately prevailed and by the end of his

London stay (August 1763) he had become a favourite with the older man.

For a time he did not have similar success with his father. Lord Auchinleck had been told of the Harvest Journal and was 'Surprised that a lad of sense and come of age should be so childish as keep a register of his follies'. He received 'a fresh mortification' with publication of the letters between his son and Erskine; and was given 'vast pain' on being told that at Springkell 'you had given yourself up to mimicry... the lowest and meanest kind of wit'. So, on 30 May 1763, he wrote to James intimating that at one stage, he 'had determined to abandon' him, 'from the principle that it is better to snuff a candle out than leave it to stink in a socket'. This is strong stuff, and no doubt it would have been stronger if Lord Auchinleck had known about Jean, Louisa and 'Signor Gonorrhoea'. However, Boswell's mother interceded with his father and a compromise was struck. He was to study law for some months at Utrecht and was to be allowed to travel in Germany and France at least. He was 'to be more on his guard for the future against mimicry, journals, and publications'. Little did Lord Auchinleck realise that it would be due to just such activities that the lasting fame of his son would be achieved.

At the beginning of August 1763, Boswell wrote to Temple: 'Tomorrow morning at 4 o'clock, I set out upon my travels... I am going far away and for a long time...' To his astonishment and deep gratification, Dr Johnson agreed to see him on his way to Harwich, where he was to embark for Holland. On 5 August, the two friends stayed overnight at an inn in Colchester, where the older man, observing a moth tormenting itself with a bright candle flame, made the famous observation: 'That creature was its own tormentor, and I believe its name was Boswell.' Thus, admonished but resolute, and seen on to his packet-boat by the most famous literary figure in England, the young Boswell set out on his travels abroad.

Boswell was based in Utrecht from August 1763 to mid-June 1764. The Dutch sojourn started on a very low note. Installed in a 'high bedroom with old furniture, where I had to sit and be fed by myself', opposite the cathedral where bells 'at every hour... played a dreary psalm tune... a deep melancholy seized upon me. I groaned with the idea of living all winter in so shocking a place... I sunk quite into despair. I thought that... I should grow mad... I went out to the street, and even in public, could not refrain from groaning and weeping bitterly. I said always: "Poor Boswell! Is it come to this?"' As we have seen, the Boswell temperament was mercurial. Clearly, what we have here is a reaction to the carefree nine months spent in London and a heavy bout of homesickness. Not perhaps for Edinburgh and

Cathedral Square, Utrecht,
in the mid-eighteenth century.

Auchinleck, but certainly for London and convivial companions left behind. He wrote to Dr Johnston seeking solace, but the good doctor ignored his complaints. As often happens, a few weeks reconciled him to his situation. He took comfort from Johnsonian words of wisdom in the *Rambler*. He drew up an 'Inviolable Plan – to be read over frequently', in which he enjoined himself to be sober, studious and restrained. What is more surprising, he largely kept to it. He worked hard at law and language. His French improved to such an extent that he could enjoy high society at The Hague over the Christmas season. He was chaste, largely temperate and quite un-Boswellian.

Poem: Sunday, 1 April 1764:

To solid studies I my time will give
And as a decent worthy fellow live.
I'll be the honest Laird of Auchinleck
And from my friends and neighbours have respect.

Belle de Zuylen [Zélide]
(1740 - 1805), aged about 26.

His father, back in Scotland, was greatly relieved: 'My dear Son, Your letter of 7th of October (1763)… gave me uncommon satisfaction and I now bless God that I have the prospect of having comfort in you and support from you and that you will tread in the footsteps of the former Jameses, who, in this family, have been remarkably useful.' This to the 'candle' he was tempted to snuff out, only a few months before.

Of course, this was not the whole story. Once the young man (still only twenty-three) had found his feet and his new tongue, he began to move in society. Thanks to introductions from his father and from Lord Hailes he was able to socialise with the local gentry and nobility. He paid chaste court to a noble young Dutch widow. Tuesday, 21 February 1764: 'Up early and to the ramparts to watch her pass': 'She looked angelic and that glimpse was ravishing… You was quite torn with love.'

Of more lasting significance was his friendship, his near love affair, with Belle De Zuylen. Twenty-three-years of age, daughter of a noble, ancient, Dutch family, and possessed of a formidable intellect, Isabella Van Tuyll was probably the most remarkable woman Boswell was ever to meet. She emerges from the correspondence like the cynical Marquise in *Les Liaisons*

Dangereuses. She was able to view herself, her emotions and her ambitions with detachment. She was prepared to discuss, with the utmost candour, love and its limitations; marriage and sexual morality. In a sense, she and Boswell were soul mates. Here was a vivacious, presentable, intelligent young man in search of the world. Here was an attractive, intriguing, eligible young woman, prepared to counter his every foil and foible with forcibly expressed ideas of her own. Boswell was smitten, yet repulsed. What a wife this would be! But what a trial! Finally, he concluded (and wrote to her after he had left Utrecht): 'I would not be married to you to be a King. I know myself and I know you. And from all probability of reasoning, I am very certain that if we were married together, it would not be long before we should both be very miserable. My wife must be a character directly opposite to my dear Zélide, except in affection, in honesty and in good humour. You may depend upon me as a friend... But I love you and would wish to contribute to your happiness.' La Belle Zélide, as she styled herself, seemed not too put out by this conclusion, although half in love herself. She went on to become the formidable Madame de Charrière, centre of a brilliant literary circle of her own and the focus of on-going literary interest to this day. Not, perhaps, the ideal mistress for the Boswell households at Auchinleck and in the Edinburgh of the 1770s.

All this time, Boswell continued to correspond with his father and his friends in Edinburgh, principally Lord Hailes and John Johnston. The last had been appointed Boswell's man of affairs at home. One of the affairs that he had to attend to was that of Boswell's illegitimate son, Charles, who had been born to Peggy Doig shortly after Boswell had left for London. Not at all dismayed by this development, Boswell had made some financial provision for the child and even harboured ideas of having the boy schooled in England: 'where his parentage shall not be known, as the scoffing of his companions might break his spirit.' Alas, this was not to be.

At the beginning of March 1764, Johnston wrote that the little boy had died. Boswell seems to have been genuinely affected by this. He described himself as 'distressed and sunk', 'faint and gloomy'. Mawkishly, perhaps, he penned in his exercise book (8 March 1764):

Affliction strange, but, ah, how very keen!
I weep for him whom I have never seen.
For in my heart the warm affection dwelt
For I a father's tender fondness felt.

George Keith
(c. 1693 - 1778), the exiled
tenth Earl Marischal
of Scotland.

Other news from Scotland was good. At the beginning of June the young man received

> *a large packet of letters, one from my Lord Marischal, informing me that I was to accompany him to Berlin, one from my father to the same purpose, and letters from my Scots and London bankers with a credit upon Berlin of £30 a month. Never was a man happier than I this morning. I was now to travel with a venerable Scots nobleman who had passed all his life abroad, had known intimately Kings and great men of all kinds, and could introduce me with the greatest advantage at courts. A multitude of rich ideas filled my imagination.*

By the middle of the month, Boswell had bade farewell to Zélide and to 'dull Utrecht'. As he wrote on 11 June to Johnston: 'I have passed nine months in Holland to rational purpose, and to the satisfaction of my worthy father. And now… as a reward for my behaviour… my Lord Marischal is so good as to take me with him to Germany… All is well and if I am not happy, it must be owing to a disturbed mind… Go, my friend, by yourself to Arthur's Seat, think of me in distant regions... ' Finally, 18 June: 'I took leave of my house in which I have had such an infinity of ideas. At seven we set out in a coach and four... '

The trio in the coach which lumbered eastwards from Utrecht towards Hanover and Berlin could scarcely have been more diverse. First, of course, our subject, anxious to progress his adventures. 'My blood circulated just as briskly as in my days of youth' (He was still only twenty-three!). Second, the venerable Earl Marischal Keith. And third, the latter's adopted daughter, one Madame Froment.

George Keith (1693-1778), the hereditary Great Marischal of Scotland, was the veteran hero of the 1715 Jacobite Rebellion. He and his brother, James, had accordingly been exiled from Britain and deprived of their family estates in Scotland. Both brothers had distinguished careers in the service of Continental rulers, principally Catherine of Russia, and Frederick of Prussia. The Lord Marischal had served Frederick as Ambassador in Paris and Madrid, and was Governor of Neuchâtel (now part of Switzerland). He had dissociated himself from the Stuart cause prior to the disastrous Rebellion of 1745 and had latterly been restored to his estates. For a time he had resided again in Scotland but had lately been recalled to the service of his royal master Frederick. He was thus one of the most distinguished Scotsmen and Europeans of his day.

His brother, James, had risen to the rank of Field Marshal in the Prussian service and had been killed on the field of Hochkirch in 1758. In the course of his campaigning, he had rescued the young Turkish daughter of a Chief Janissary during the Siege of Otchakoff in 1733. The girl, Emetulla, had been adopted by the Keiths and was now married to a Frenchman resident in Berlin. Now about thirty-nine years of age, Madame was said to be languid and taciturn, but with the ebullient Boswell as a travelling companion she soon started to chatter. After a few days' travelling and suppers tête-à-tête, Boswell even contemplated the possibility of Turkish delight. 'She seemed too indolent in body, and too vivacious in mind to be a very rigid lady.' Shades of Lord Kames and Jean!

Boswell had trouble with the 'plain old Scots nobleman', as he described the Earl Marischal. From time to time, the statesman would condescend to chat, for example to deplore the British government's policy in reducing the Highlands and trying to make the gallant clansmen into Lowlanders. Generally, though, he kept Boswell at his distance. The latter was reminded of his own father's demeanour. But eventually he did win the old man round. Just before he left Berlin to continue his travels,

Boswell sent the Earl one of his masterly letters that so often gained him access to the confidence and affection of others. In this (dated 2 September 1764) he mildly upbraids his eminent senior for using him so coolly: 'My dear Lord! Why do I see you so seldom? Is it not hard that one who values your conversation so much should have it so little?' He goes on to request the Marischal to engineer matters to allow him to 'hear the King talk', and to seek his assistance in persuading his father to allow him to continue his travels to Italy. In his second objective Boswell succeeded and permission was eventually given. The Earl Marischal even offered him funds if need be. But as to meeting the King, the young traveller suffered a rare failure. Not even Boswell's blandishments could secure an audience with Frederick. 'I am quite out of conceit with monarchy' he noted in his diary (22 September 1764).

Otherwise, the German trip was a great success. He was taken up to an extent by the court of the Duke of Brunswick. He had several meetings with the Duke's heir, Prince Ferdinand. He danced and chatted with the Princess, George III's sister:

> No sooner did the amiable Princess perceive me, than she came up to me with a smile so celestial and said, 'Mr Boswell, let us finish our minuet.' Accordingly I danced with her Royal Highness, who danced extremely well. We made a very fine English minuet – or British if you please, for it was a Scots gentleman and an English lady that performed it. What a group of fine ideas had I! I was dancing with a Princess; with the grand-daughter of King George whose birthday I have so often helped to celebrate at Old Edinburgh; with the daughter of the Prince of Wales, who patronised Thomson and other votaries of science and the muse; with the sister of George III, my sovereign. I mark this variety to show how my imagination can enrich an object, so that I have double pleasure when I am well. I was noble to be in such a frame. I said to the Princess 'Madam, I return your Royal Highness a thousand thanks for the honour you have done me. This will serve me to talk of to my tenants as long as I live.

At a magnificent court dinner one Sunday (12 August 1764) he 'had the utmost pleasure of contrast by considering at this hour is assembled Auchinleck kirk, and many a whine and many a sad look is found therein.'

At Berlin, too, he did well. He was presented to the Queen of Prussia, in whom Frederick apparently took little interest (another avenue thwarted). He had comfortable lodgings with the family of the Prefect of Police. He jaunted about the city and its environs with another young Scot, a Lieutenant MacPherson. The two of them one evening dressed up as Scots Highlanders ('Messrs McDonald and McIntosh'), to play a joke on the Earl Marischal. 'His Lordship made us welcome. We stood just within his door, bowing much. He cried: "Come in gentlemen, come in." He advanced and immediately knew us and asked us how cows sold. He took our joke in good part. We marched home again.' There were other very different military encounters. At one party, a French officer took grave exception to Boswell's aspersions on the French and called him a 'scoundrel'. A duel was only narrowly averted by a typical Boswellian combination of braggadocio and grovelling. On another front, the year's chastity came to an abrupt close thanks to a visit of a soldier's wife who came to Boswell's lodgings at eight o'clock one morning to sell him chocolate. 'I toyed with her and found she was with child. Oho! A safe piece. Into my closet... to bed directly. In a minute, over. I rose cool and astonished, half angry, half laughing. I sent her off. Bless me, have I now committed adultery?' All in all, life's rich tapestry continued to unfold for our Grand Tourist.

Boswell's stay in Berlin and neighbourhood lasted almost three months. At last, realising that he was not, after all, destined to meet King Frederick even by dint of throwing himself at his feet, Boswell took an affectionate leave of the Earl Marischal and 'my poor Turk with regret ', and set off south to visit some of the other German courts. With him, he had a friendly letter from the Earl asking him to convey his regards to the great Rousseau.

To the modern European traveller, Boswell's onward plan of progress southwards through the German princely states seems bizarre. Basically, he was en route to Switzerland, hoping to meet Rousseau and his arch-rival Voltaire. But he planned a leisurely tour of some weeks, with frequent stops at the principalities of those rulers who interested him or to whose courts he had an introduction. He there hoped to be received, entertained and sent on his way with further introductions. We are, of course, still in 1764, when this part of Europe was a patchwork of small states of varying degrees of autonomy. It was the twilight of aristocratic times, where even the tiniest principality had its palace and its retinue. Just the thing for 'Baron Boswell' as he now decided he had to become. Journal, 30 September 1764: 'I think it proper to take the title of Baron in Germany, as I have just the same right to it as the good gentry whom I see around me.'

The courts and the courtiers were of a variegated and cosmopolitan character. Again and again, Boswell met relations and friends of nobles or officials whom he had already met in Holland or Berlin. Many were well travelled, and some had even been to Scotland. M Froment, the husband of 'the Turk', had found Scotsmen over-familiar: 'A fellow there will call you by your first name: "Oh, Jack" – and perhaps give you a kick in the backside.' The Scots ladies had been grievously dull and stood around yawning all the time. But, whatever the repute of the Scots, the magic name of the Earl Marischal generally ensured Boswell a good reception. So, he hunted with a Prince of Anhalt, was presented (in a home-made uniform) at the court of the Elector of Saxony as 'an officer in Loudon's regiment', and personally petitioned the Margrave of Baden-Durlach for an award of his Order. Alas, no ribbon and star: but a brave attempt.

It should not be thought that our traveller was purely an opportunist. Boswell could be very good company. By this time his French was fluent and his German passable. Moreover, the courts impress as being provincial and boring in the main. The company may well have been relieved to have the presence of a lively young stranger in their midst for a few days. But he did not impress everywhere.

In the pocket state of the Prince of Zerbst at Coswig, he was arrested on suspicion of being a spy for enquiring as to the size of the Prince's army (180 men as it transpired). 'I… marched with all the formal composure of a state prisoner' He was regarded with some suspicion by the Grand Marechal of the Landgrave of Hesse-Kassel. 'A foreign adventurer' who had claimed to be the son of the Duke of Hamilton, had recently tricked the court out of clothes and equipment. Boswell (nonplussed): 'Sir, if one receives such a man as that, one deserves to be taken in'! And all was not magnificence. Between stops, Boswell and Jacob, his servant, usually travelled with the lumbering post-wagons and had sometimes to do with straw for a bed on an inn floor. Some fellow sleepers were openly derisive: 'How goes it with the Baron: some roaring Germans in a drunken tone still rudely bawl'd,' as he wryly recorded.

As to his behaviour: nigh impeccable. To Lord Kames (who would *not* have approved of the 'Baron' appendage), he wrote (27 September 1764): 'I am every day becoming more temperate in mind… upon the whole I think myself a good deal improved'. And, apart from a couple of forays between the thighs (only) of the 'easy street girls' of Dresden (for the health of the loins), he does seem to have behaved himself. His resolution not to err again, save perhaps with 'a healthy Swiss girl', was fortified by having his pocket picked and having to confess all to his long-suffering servant.

Jean-Jaques Rousseau
(1712 - 78), Philosopher
and man of letters.
Received Boswell kindly
on his travels.

As he travelled on, Scotland was not forgotten. The old town of Leipzig had high houses as in Edinburgh. The scenery in Neuchâtel reminded him of the Pass of Killiecrankie. He even astonished some venerable German professors in Leipzig by declaiming a passage from the Declaration of Arbroath from an old Scots book in a library there. 'They were struck with the noble sentiments of liberty of the old Scots and they expressed their regret at the shameful Union. I felt true patriot sorrow... alas, poor Scotland!' Somehow, it was easier to be patriotic at a distance.

Big game now loomed in the sights of our literary scalp hunter. His targets were two very different types of men.

Voltaire was the most celebrated literary figure in Europe. He was seventy years of age, rich, famous and living in some splendour in his French chateau at Ferney, a mile or two from the Swiss border. In the late 1720s he had spent three years in England and still spoke fluent English,when he had a mind to do so. His mind was very much his own and his waspish wit renowned and feared. Unlike his arch-rival Rousseau, he had the ear and encouragement of the establishment.

The fame of Jean-Jacques Rousseau was of a different type: notoriety better describes it. In his brilliant works he had dared to challenge the existing social and religious order and had been hounded from this territory to that. He had found a precarious (if temporary) home at Motiers in the Principality of Neuchâtel, where the Earl Marischal as Governor had afforded him some protection. He was fifty years of age, unwell with a urinary complaint, and increasingly paranoid. To be received by either one of these fierce lions would be difficult. To be entertained and chatted to by both would be nigh miraculous.

Undeterred, our young hero set to work. A letter of introduction which the Earl Marischal had given him to Rousseau would almost certainly have ensured him an audience. But Boswell decided to be received on his own merits. And received he was by means of a carefully drafted and redrafted letter ("a masterpiece'), carefully couched to arouse the philosopher's curiosity. As Rousseau himself later described to a correspondent (20 December 1764):

> *In the first letter he wrote me, he told me that he was a man 'of singular merit'. I was curious to see a man who spoke of himself in such a fashion and I found that he had told me the truth. In his youth he got his head confused with a smattering of harsh Calvinist theology, and he still retains, because of it, a troubled soul and gloomy notions… He is a convalescent whom the least relapse will infallibly destroy. I should have been interested in him even if he had not been recommended to me by the Lord Marischal.*

In short, then, Boswell introduced himself, and was made cautiously welcome. He took little time to gain the philosopher's confidence. Half by imposition, half by guile, he saw Rousseau on five separate occasions. He gave him a *Sketch of his Life,* for his observations. He laid siege to Thérèse, his housekeeper/mistress. They, all three, dined simply and well together in the kitchen of Rousseau's house. 'There was something singularly agreeable in this scene.' The parting with Rousseau was tender and sincere. And Thérèse was promised (and got) a garnet necklace.

On, then, via Lausanne and Geneva to Ferney. Access there was not so complicated: by way of a letter of introduction from a mutual friend whom Boswell had met in Holland. But the first brief meeting with the famous septuagenarian was far from sufficient for Boswell. So again, a letter. This time to the niece of the great man, with whom Boswell had dined. 'I address myself to you Madam, as to the friend of the stranger…' The gates to Geneva shut at five you see, and as she knows, her uncle starts to

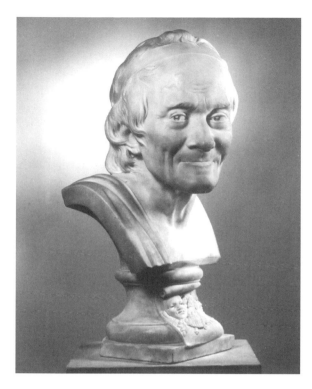

Voltaire (1694 - 1778):
the waspish philosopher,
interviewed by Boswell,
(bust by J A Houdon).

'shine' late in the evening. So, 'even a bed upon two chairs in the bedchamber of your maid, whom I saw the other day, would suffice!' The household at Ferney was amused, and an invitation was issued by the great man himself. A further two days of literary talk then followed, even though M Voltaire was not quite so easy to put to the question as the sage of Motiers. For example, it would be useless to have a school of painting in Scotland, because one cannot paint with cold feet! M Boswell had plans to travel to the Western Isles with Dr Johnson? Voltaire hoped they wouldn't mind if he didn't come! But even the old sceptic appears to have been intrigued and amused by his visitor. He was persuaded to speak English for Boswell and did so in the rumbustious fashion of the 1720s. 'He swore bloodily as was the fashion when he was in England. He hummed a ballad; he repeated nonsense. Then he talked about the Constitution with a noble enthusiasm... At last we came upon religion.' As Boswell remarked with exultation in a letter to Temple (28 December 1764), '... was this not an interesting scene? Would a journey from Scotland to Ferney have been too much to obtain such a remarkable interview?' Once more, posterity has reason to be grateful to Boswell for his persistence as he took extensive notes of his conversations with Voltaire. So we have a

The interior of St Peter's, Rome , by Giovanni Panini, c.1740.

unique and contemporary insight into the mind of the venerable cynic.

But enough of the literary chase. On with the travels. On 1 January 1765 Boswell set out from Geneva 'at eleven in a chaise mounted so high before, that I was thrown back like a Bishop in his studying-chair. All the chaises for passing the Alps are hung in this way. I jogged on, mightly deliberate.' Boswell, in role of Hannibal, was off to conquer Italy.

His journey from Geneva over the Alps to Turin took him a week. Although it was the height of winter, the passage seems to have been uncomplicated. The prospect 'was horribly grand and the snow sometimes six feet deep', but our traveller arrived in Italy unscathed. He later wrote to Rousseau that he 'carried over the Alps ideas of the most rigorous morality'. If this were so, they were soon dissipated in the relaxed moral clime of Italy.

On his first evening in Turin, still unwashed from his journey, Boswell went to the opera. 'The superb theatre struck me much, and the boxes full of ladies and gallants talking to each other, quite Italy.' Within a week he was so taken with what he perceived to be the spirit of the place that he was laying siege to no fewer than three Italian countesses. Rejected ultimately by all, he travelled, smarting, on to Milan. To be fair to our hero, he was still only twenty-four, he had been largely chaste since leaving London about eighteen months before and he was only an apprentice rake

John Stuart (1744 - 1814),
Lord Mountstuart, eldest son
of Lord Bute. Boswell's
travelling companion and
unwilling patron.

in a land of professionals. However, as one earlier Boswellian (Geoffrey Scott) deftly put it: 'Boswell was pedantic in Holland, princely in Germany, philosophic in Switzerland' but was definitely to be 'amorous in Italy'.

It is not our purpose to follow the young James in to every chapel and bordello, or to attend every dinner and conversazione that would fill the next ten months or so. To know Boswell we must know that he spent this time in Italy and that it profoundly affected him and and broadened his outlook. We should know that he was presented to the Pope and kissed his slipper 'rich and gold'; that he had an attractive portrait painted of himself and that he renewed his acquaintance and correspondence with John Wilkes. From the Scottish perspective, we should be interested to learn that he became acquainted with the secretary of Prince Charles Edward Stuart, Andrew Lumisden: 'a learned, pretty, honourable man'. Boswell also spent some weeks travelling in the illustrious company of young Lord Mountstuart, son of the Earl of Bute, lately British Prime Minister. Boswell-like, he veered madly in his attitude towards the young nobleman: from the sycophantic, to the rude, to the sentimental. The mark that Boswell left on the young Lord and his travelling companions was not a commendable one. On a shared nocturnal foray, both young men were (via the same pretty Venetian dancer) bit by the same venereal tartar: 'Pretty doings!' as Boswell put it.

Finally, and probably to the supplicant's surprise, he was indeed granted the favours of a real Italian countess. By now it was August 1765 and in Sienna. Addressing his suit first to a former mistress of Lord Mountstuart and being rejected by her, Boswell then transferred his affections to the wife of the Capitano di Popolo, one Girolama, in her mid-thirties and mother of four. Girolama or 'Moma' as she was familiarly known, was spirited and demanding and almost proved too much for the young cavalier. After a fortnight he had to insist on taking his leave. "She shed tears without affectation and promised fidelity.' He promised 'eternal friendship' and left 'quite in confusion'. An emotion tempered with relief, one suspects.

By now (almost three years after his son's departure), Lord Auchinleck's purse and patience were wearing thin. 'Your conduct astonishes and amazes me' he was to write. 'I have wrote letters on the back of letters to you, telling you to come home. Whether any of these have reached you, I cannot say.' The father's indignation was well founded, as James had already spent over £500 on his Italian trip. This was 'a vast deal of money', as Lord Auchinleck put it, 'which is much beyond what my income can afford, and much beyond what the sons of gentlemen near double my estate have spent on such a tour…'. But there was one thing more to do, and that was to make the journey which would ensure Boswell's fame.

In the published account of his *Journal of a Tour to Corsica* (1768), Boswell summarised the reason for his visit thus:

> *Having resolved to pass some years abroad for my instruction and entertainment, I conceived a design of visiting the Island of Corsica. I wished for something more than just a common course of what is called the tour of Europe; and Corsica occurred to me as a place which nobody else had seen, and where I should find what was to be seen nowhere else, people actually fighting for liberty and forming themselves from a poor, inconsiderable oppressed nation into a flourishing and independent state.*

Of course, as was usual with our traveller, the facts were not quite so straightforward. One of the topics of his conversations with Rousseau had been a suggestion made on the islanders' behalf that the philosopher

The Island of Corsica
in 1769

might frame them a constitution. Boswell had half-jokingly offered to be his envoy. Rousseau had tartly riposted that Boswell would perhaps rather be King! When a visit to the island became feasible, Boswell had sought a letter of introduction from Rousseau, which the latter had supplied. Armed with this, an elaborate British passport (in case he was captured by pirates) and letters of recommendation from the Sardinian Consul, Boswell set sail in a 'bark' from Leghorn, bound for Capo Corso, in the extreme north of the island. It was now the beginning of October 1765. Boswell had reason to be apprehensive. The Corsicans were in a state of insurrection against the occupying Genoans and their French allies. No British gentleman had ever visited the island's rugged and wild interior or met the Corsican leader. Our young man, shortly to be twenty-five, was, however, an optimist.

In fact, the trip was a great success. Boswell found the Corsicans friendly and hospitable. He successfully negotiated the hair-raising mountain tracks with the aid of local guides and mules. He traversed practically the whole length of the island – over 100 rugged miles. And

General Pasquale de Paoli (1725 - 1807). The Corsican leader who was host to Boswell on his visit to the Island.

finally, in the southern town of Sollacaro, he was ushered into the presence of the Patriots' leader, the famous Pasquale de Paoli. Here at last was a hero: the latest in a long line, stretching from his father, through Lord Kames, Dr Johnson, Rousseau and Voltaire.

At first, the hero was highly suspicious of the young Scot. Was he an imposter? Worse, could he be 'an espy'? He certainly seemed keen to note everything down! If he was genuine, what was he doing in Corsica? Did he represent the British government in an oblique way? Naturally, Boswell was not inclined to lessen the importance of his mission. So, when he had gained the great man's confidence, he gladly accepted the armed escorts and the generous entertainments supplied. King of Corsica he might not be, but friend of the uncrowned King he decidedly was.

Boswell's published journal of his tour is highly readable. Much of it consists of his impressions of the heroic and noble Paoli. But there are charming and valuable observations too, on the island and the islanders. It seems likely that Boswell found many of the better qualities of the Scottish Highlanders in the Corsicans. They were proud, brave and intensely patriotic. They were hardy and passionate. They would despatch an

Arrival of the Diligence at Paris. Some 35 years after Boswell's travels, conditions were still primitive. (Painting by Boilly, c 1803).

enemy without a qualm but none of them would act as hangman, even to save his own life. Boswell entertained them with Scots airs on his flute and sang them 'Hearts of Oak': *'Cuore di quercia',* cried they, *'bravo Inglese!'* After enjoying the hospitality of the Patriots' leader for a week or so, Boswell left, crowned with glory, bearing the good wishes of Paoli to all those sympathetic to his cause, and accompanied by a large dog presented to him as a farewell gift. He was also accompanied by a developing malarial fever, and toes which had suffered greatly from the rigours of his travels through the mountains. His fever became quite acute and delayed his departure. For a time, he was in the care of the French commander of the island's garrison – such was the ambivalent state of relations between the Corsicans and their occupiers. Unfortunately, the amiable laissez-faire atmosphere was not to last. In 1769, the French resolved to take over the island by force and did so. Paoli, Boswell's hero, had to escape to exile in England. Rousseau's constitution was not to be required. But Boswell was to bring the island and its cause to the attention of the world.

Recovered from his 'ague', but still suffering from his feet, Boswell eventually sailed into Genoa after a rough and interrupted passage from the island. There were love letters from Moma and letters of rebuke from trary, when they had concluded the last peace with France, they published a proclamation, declaring it high treason for any British subject, to affist the Corficans; the rebellious Corficans [xxiv. 674.]; — and for this proclamation the then prime minifter of England was feverely cenfured by the daring Sieur Wilkes, whose North-Briton made fuch an uproar. —— The gazettes of late have talked a great deal of a certain M. Bofwell, a Scots gentleman, who has been in Corfica. It was at firft rumoured that he was a defperate adventurer, whofe real name was *Macdonald*, and who had ferved during the laft war in North America; but it has fince appeared that he is a gentleman of fortune upon his travels, a friend of the celebrated John James Roulleau, who is an enthufiaft for the Corficans, and has been honoured with the title of their legiflator. We do not give credit to the reports of M. Bofwell's having had inftructions from his court to treat with Signior de Paoli, but we are in great hopes,

cult to be explained, is Mr Bofwell's having failed almoft before any body knew of his intention. He carried all the appearance of a gentleman travelling for his amufement; paffed fome time with the Count de Marbeuf, commander in chief of the French troops in Corfica; and afterwards went to Genoa, where he ftaid about a week, and feemed free and unconcerned, as if he had nothing to do with ftate-difputes. People in this part of the world are curious to know what will really be the confequence of Mr Bofwell's tour to Corfica."

" *London, Jan.* 11. When Mr Bofwell was prefented to the General de Paoli, he paid this compliment to the Corficans: " Sir, I am upon my travels, and have lately vifited Rome. I am come from feeing the ruins of one brave and free people: I now fee the rife of another."

Extracts from *Scots Magazine* of 1766 recording Boswell's exploits in Corisca.

Lord Auchinleck. As the voyager put it: 'What variety! Dined with immense pleasure.' Now it was time for the homeward stretch. Journal, 11 December 1765: 'Scotland stared me full in the face, but seemed comfortable. I wished to be home.'

Once on the road, and compared to his earlier leisurely progress, Boswell did not delay. By 21 December he was in Marseilles, where he visited the galley slaves and a Mlle. Susette. He spent Christmas in Avignon and was entertained by two prominent Jacobite exiles, the Earl of Dunbar and his sister, Lady Inverness. They greeted Boswell with old-fashioned Scots courtliness and were full of anecdotes of the 1715 Rebellion of fifty years before. 'We recalled the ancient days of Scots glory.' After a brief deviation to visit Montpellier and Nîmes, the traveller bore north once more toward Lyons. En route, he was plagued by his sore feet, his querulous servant Jacob (who had been with him since Holland) and his undisciplined dog. The latter, Corsican free spirit, kept dashing off in search of food and was finally lost, near Auxerre. After a last round of recriminations and counter-complaints, Jacob was paid off in Lyons. Journal, Wednesday, 18 December 1765:

Jacob said, 'I believe, sir, that you have been badly brought up. You have not the manners of a nobleman. Your heart is too open.' I

*confessed to him that I was two and twenty before I had a servant.
Said he, 'The son of a gentleman ought to be accustomed early to
command a servant, but reasonably, and never to joke with them;
because each must live in his state accordingly to his quality. You,
sir, would live just like a peasant. And you force a servant to speak in
a way he shouldn't, because you torment him with questions. You
want to get to the bottom of things... I hope, sir, you will not take this
in bad part.'*

And, after several disconcerting encounters with provincial 'surgeons', the sore toes were finally attended to in Paris.

Paris meant a renewal of acquaintance with John Wilkes and a somewhat icy meeting with Horace Walpole, 'a lean genteel man', who looked on Rousseau as a 'mountebank with great parts'. That philosopher had, meantime, been expelled from Neuchâtel and had gone to England at the invitation of David Hume. His consort Thérèse was still in Paris. Who better to conduct her to her illustrious master than our traveller?

But first, a real blow: quite the heaviest of the three years' absence from home. Monday, 27 January 1766: 'At Wilkes: saw *St James Chronicle* of 18th January, Mother's death. Quite stunned: tried to dissipate [grief]. Dined Dutch Ambassadors: much of Corsica. At six, Mme Huquet's, as in fever, Constance elegant.' Boswell was deeply affected by the death of his pious, gentle mother, but it speaks volumes for the contradictions in his character when one realises what the other items in the entry signify. 'Mme Huquet's was a brothel, and the elegant Constance, a courtesan.

Lord Auchinleck had also been seriously ill and a letter arriving within a day or so made it very clear that he was shattered by his wife's death. The event also temporarily softened his attitude towards the errant James. After describing the sad circumstances of the demise, the father finishes: 'Farewell, my dear Jamie, may God bless and preserve you.' The new note of tenderness was not to last. As he approached London, Boswell forwarded various items for the London and Edinburgh papers, dealing in a light-hearted fashion with his visit to Corsica and his dealings with Paoli. For example, the *Scots Magazine* of January 1766 devotes almost a page to an account of the visit (authored by Boswell himself of course), and concludes: 'People in this part of the world are curious to know what will really be the consequence of Mr Boswell's tour to Corsica.' Not surprisingly, Lord Auchinleck was enraged to see the family name bandied about in the press once more, and at such a time.

> already received a firſt reading in the H——
> of L.
>   This day the Court of Seſſion roſe:
> Their next term commences the 12th of
> June next.
>   On Thurſday laſt arrived here from his
> travels, James Boſwell, Eſq; younger of
> Auchinleck.
>   The weather here, for ſome days paſt,
> has been remarkably fine; and as mild, as
> uſually in the beginning of May.——We hear,

Boswell's home-coming as recorded in *The Edinburgh Advertiser* of Tuesday,
March 11 1766.

All this was ahead. Boswell had in the meantime left Paris with Thérèse, to deliver her to her master in England. At this point, pages of the journal have been removed by the family at some later date, with the note 'Reprehensible Passage' appended. That the passage was indeed reprehensible, there can be little doubt, because the journal narrative resumes at Dover: Wednesday, 12 February: 'Yesterday morning had gone to bed very early and had done it once: thirteen in all. Was really affectionate to her.' So, having left London in the company of Dr Johnson and full of noble ideas, the traveller is returning, two and a half years later, having taken advantage of the middle-aged mistress of another hero. Ah, Boswell! That mission, at least, was duly discharged the next day when Boswell delivered Thérèse to Rousseau at Chiswick: 'Quanta oscula etc. He seemed so oldish and weak, you no longer had your enthusiasm for him.' That same day, Boswell was reunited with Dr Johnson who hugged the young man to him 'like a sack'. Even the great man at first seemed 'not so immense as before, but it came back'. One is glad that it did: two idols shattered in one day would be a high price to pay, even for two and a half years of eventful travelling.

Two final matters of significance before Scotland reclaimed the traveller. On 18 February Boswell was presented at court. The King (George III) remarked, 'Lately come over?' 'All he said,' noted Boswell wryly. And on the 23rd, a more meaningful audience with the famous statesman William Pitt, then in opposition. Boswell wished to have his help in a campaign to enlist British government support for Corsica. Pitt was sympathetic but non-committal. He reaffirmed his enthusiasm for 'the cause of liberty', and graciously dismissed the emissary.

There was little now to keep Boswell in London. At the beginning of March Boswell again took the road north. One of the first things that struck him about his native land was the harshness of the Scots accent. The *Edinburgh Advertiser* for Tuesday, 11 March 1766 has the following item: 'On Thursday last, arrived here from his travels, James Boswell, Esquire, younger of Auchinleck.' It goes on to record: 'The weather here, for some days past, has been remarkably fine, and is mild, as usually in the beginning of May. We hear, that oat-feed, in the low parts of the country, is generally over.' So, too, was the Grand Tour of our hero.

CHAPTER 6

Professional Life and Marriage:
1766-1769

There is no extant domestic record of Boswell's homecoming. It was the end of the winter law term and the household would shortly have been off to Auchinleck. Boswell's mother had been dead barely two months. That sad event must have cast a gloom over what would have otherwise been a joyous return after more than three years' absence. Lord Auchinleck's affection towards his eldest son was often tempered with exasperation, particularly with the Corsican campaign in full swing before the traveller reached home. His brother David put it thus: '... although he seems to take little satisfaction in his sons when they are with him, yet when they are absent, he wishes constantly for them and thinks their presence would enliven him. This, I well remember, was the case before you came from abroad, and yet, how soon after your arrival did he grow displeased with you!'

For the moment, though, there were two great projects to take up Boswell's time and energy. First, he had to finish his legal studies, to enable him to pass Advocate. Second, he had to write his *Account of Corsica*. The quiet and measured life at Auchinleck was ideal for these purposes and it is from there that we next hear of him. In a letter to Temple, written at the end of April 1766, there is not a word about his homecoming (possibly he had described it in an unrecovered letter). Instead we are treated to pages of passion declared for Euphemia Bruce, daughter of the Auchinleck overseer. Even the robust, amorous experiences of the traveller with the Italian countess and the French housekeeper had failed to destroy the romantic. Fortunately for all, a

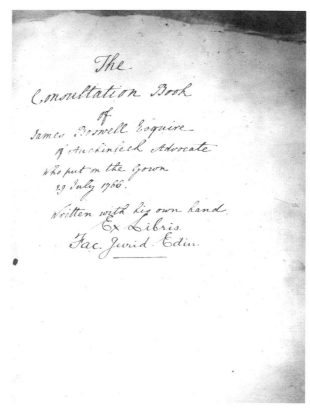

The.

Consultation Book

of

James Boswell Esquire

of Auchinleck Advocate

who put on the Gown

29 July 1766.

Written with his own hand.

Ex Libris.

Fac. Jurid. Edin.

Title page of the Consultation Book in which the proud new advocate recorded his cases and fees (see also chapter 8).

month's holiday had been arranged for the family to take the waters at Moffat. There awaited a more serious proposition. But all in good time.

The studies proved successful. Returned to Edinburgh for the start of the summer law term, Boswell passed his examination in Scots law on 11 July 1766. On the 26th, he underwent his public examination. This entailed his presenting a short Latin thesis to the assembled Faculty of Advocates. The intrant was then questioned in Latin on his chosen theme by Faculty members and had to defend his subject with appropriate Latin responses. The members of Faculty then voted on whether the intrant had passed muster. Curiously, this form of Faculty examination was to survive for precisely two centuries after Boswell sat and passed it. The last such examination took place in July 1966, although by then the submitting of a thesis and the posing of the questions had become largely a formality. In any event, as recorded proudly in his own 'Consultation Book', Boswell 'put on the Gown' of Advocate on 29 July 1766 and remained in practice at the Scottish Bar for the next twenty years.

Work also proceeded apace on the *Account of Corsica*. As explained on

A N

A C C O U N T

O F

C O R S I C A,

THE JOURNAL OF A TOUR
TO THAT ISLAND;

A N D M E M O I R S O F

PASCAL PAOLI.

BY JAMES BOSWELL, Efq;

ILLUSTRATED with a New and Accurate MAP of CORSICA.

Non enim propter gloriam, divitias aut honores pugnamus, fed propter liber-
tatem folummodo, quam nemo bonus nifi fimul cum vita amittit.
Lit. Comit. et Baron. Scotiae ad Pap. A. D. 1310.

G L A S G O W,

PRINTED BY ROBERT AND ANDREW FOULIS FOR
EDWARD AND CHARLES DILLY IN THE POULTRY, LONDON;
M DCC LXVIII.

The title page of the *Account of Corsica,* published in 1768.

the title page, the work was really in two parts: the Account of the Island, and the Journal of Boswell's own Tour, together with his Memoirs of General Paoli. As it transpired, it was Boswell's account of his own travels and experiences on the island that was to catch the public imagination. As Dr Johnson put it (in a letter of 9 September 1769): 'Your "History" was copied from books; your Journal rose out of your own experience and observation. You expressed images which operated strongly upon yourself and you have impressed them with great force upon your readers. I know not whether I could name any narrative by which curiousity is better excited or better gratified.' So, during the spring and summer of 1767, Boswell scribbled industriously away at *Corsica.*

By October 1767, it was in the press and being printed by the notable Glasgow firm of R and A Foulis. The publishers were to be Messrs E & C Dilly who also published the *Life of Johnson,* as well as many works of note of the period. Moreover, the publishers paid the young author 100 guineas for the copyright: well over £10,000 at today's prices. Not only the writer expected great things of *Corsica!*

Let us revert to 1766 and to two causes célèbres current at the time of Boswell's homecoming. Both were cases then pending before the Scottish courts and both were of high interest to the Boswell family.

The first involved the prosecution of Katherine Nairn, or Ogilvie, and her brother in law, Patrick Ogilvie, for murder and incest. As would be the case today, all the elements necessary for a strong and salacious public interest were present in the case. Katherine Nairn, who was nineteen at the time of the trial, had married Thomas Ogilvie in January 1765. The allegation was that Katherine had soon tired of her new husband and had fallen in love with his brother, a dashing lieutenant of the 89th Regiment of Foot. The two were said to have formed an adulterous (and hence incestuous) association in the early part of that year and to have 'lain together' and 'abused their bodies with one another'. On the affair being discovered and the errant brother-in-law being put out of the house, it was said that the guilty couple had conspired to poison the husband by Katherine putting arsenic in his tea. The trial took place on six days in August 1765 with Lord Auchinleck as one of the presiding judges. There appears to have been ample evidence, from family and servants, of both the adultery and the poisoning and 'by great plurality of voices' the all-male jury found the couple guilty. The lieutenant was condemned to be hanged, and eventually was, on 13 November 1765. Sentence was deferred on Katherine Nairn who was pregnant. However, after giving birth to a daughter the following March, Katherine escaped from the Tolbooth Prison and fled to France, apparently disguised as a soldier. Her uncle, the future judge Sir William Nairn, is said to have been instrumental in her escape. His portrait, by Raeburn, still stares benignly across Parliament Hall. The lasting legacy for Lord Auchinleck was a severe and recurring condition of suppression of urine, thought to have arisen from his sitting for nine hours without a break during one session of the trial.

Boswell father and son were both heavily involved in another lawsuit of high general interest. This became known as the 'Douglas Cause'. It involved the representatives of the family of the Duke of Hamilton attempting to reduce the title of Archibald Douglas to the Douglas estates. The history is a somewhat complex one. The last Duke of Douglas had died in 1761 without direct heirs. His sister, Lady Jane Douglas, had eloped at the age of forty-eight with Colonel Stewart, the future laird of Grandtully. They had gone to live in France in very reduced circumstances. Lady Jane had then claimed to have had twin sons, at the age of fifty. Archibald was the survivor of the twins. He had been served as

Archibald Douglas, first Baron Douglas (1748 - 1827). The central figure in the *Douglas Cause*.

heir (i.e. legally confirmed in his title to the estate) and the current action was to try and have the service annulled.

The tale was a romantic if unlikely one. The Hamilton faction claimed that the Douglas twins had in fact been children purchased in France and produced evidence to this effect. The public interest in this squabble between the nobility was heightened by accounts of the indigent Lady Jane and her infant sons being turned away from the gates of Douglas Castle by an order of one of the Duke's associates. The case had been on-going since 1762 and, by the summer of 1767, was about to come to a head. Perhaps because he saw a parallel between his own situation as a lawful son in danger of disinheritance, Boswell became an ardent partisan for the Douglas faction. In the spring of 1767 he published *Dorando: A Spanish Tale,* a fifty-page pamphlet in which the main events and protagonists in the cause were described, thinly disguised in a Spanish context. Not only was the newly called advocate risking a finding of contempt of court for reviewing the facts in dispute in a partisan way before the court had pronounced on them, but, by poking fun at the court

Sir David Dalrymple,
Lord Hailes (1726 - 92).
Boswell's long-suffering
friend and adviser.

itself (represented as 'the Senate of Seville') and the House of Lords (as 'the Grandees of Madrid'), our pamphleteer was treading on very dangerous ground indeed. Later in the year, he also published a summary of the arguments in the case from the Douglas point of view under the title *The Essence of the Douglas Cause.*

And while the case was actually being argued before the Court of Session in June 1767, Boswell was responsible for a series of newspaper squibs about a team of shorthand writers supposedly coming up from England to note the arguments verbatim (this not being permitted by the then current court practice). The fictional team were precisely described and were daily reported to be nearing Edinburgh. It was said that they would gain admission to the court in disguise if need be… and so on. By early July, the court had had enough and the publishers of all four Edinburgh newspapers were summonsed and warned of the consequences of contempt. Boswell himself had the temerity to appear for the Edinburgh Advertiser. In later life, Boswell often wondered bitterly why he had never achieved professional preferment in his native land. Then, as now, the establishment does not enjoy being made to look foolish.

The result in the Court of Session was seven judges for the Hamilton faction and seven for Douglas. The Lord President (Dundas) had the casting vote and was for the Hamilton faction. Public uproar ensued and an appeal was made by the Douglas adherents to the 'Grandees of Madrid'. The House of Lords considered the appeal and gave judgment at the end of February 1769, reversing the decision of the Court of Session. When the news reached Edinburgh a few days later, the effect was explosive. Mobs roamed the streets celebrating the victory. Windows were smashed in houses where the occupants had failed to illuminate to mark the result. The houses of several judges were attacked and Boswell is said to have been part of a crowd who meted out this treatment to the house of his own father (even though Lord Auchinleck had been for Douglas). Later, the Lord Marischal wrote commending him on his spirit. Lord Hailes, another friend and mentor, was less pleased. He wrote Boswell an aggrieved letter complaining of the effrontery done to his house and household:

> *Had the mob satisfied themselves with breaking my windows and thrown in stones which might have murdered the family, I might have been less displeased when the first attack was over. But renewed attacks not at windows but at my door, in order to break it open, these are insults which every man of spirit and dignity must feel. I am not at liberty to suppose that you had any hand in such things directly, and I wish that you may have an opportunity of letting me know that you did not countenance the mob when in my neighbourhood and just in the street where I live; I never could ask you any more particular question, for this reason which upon recollection will suggest itself to you, that had you in an unguarded hour forgot yourself and me, and had you acknowledged it, this would have been a circumstance for proving one of the greatest insults that has been committed...*

The Douglas faction was of course delighted with the outcome. Archibald, confirmed in his estates, gave a grand birthday party at his mansion at Bothwell in July and Boswell was one of the guests of honour. After (and during) many a celebratory bumper, Boswell co-ordinated an Artillery salute. As he put it: 'We had fireworks, bonfires, and a ball, amid a crowd of country people huzzaing.' Some months later, Douglas was a witness at Boswell's wedding. He was created Lord Douglas in 1790.

Boswell (age 28) celebrating the success of his *Account of Corsica*.

But this is to anticipate. In the three and a half years between his homecoming and his eventual marriage in November 1769, Boswell pursued innumerable matrimonial schemes. He would have an English lady, a Scotch lass, a rich heiress, one who would have him for himself, and so on. Most of these schemes were recounted, in sometimes tedious detail, in correspondence with his friend Temple, now a clergyman in a modest living in Devon. It is enough for us to know that an eligible heiress, Catherine Blair of Adamton, of whom Lord Auchinleck approved, eventually turned him down: '… a damned jilt. What a risk I have run!' And that the sixteen-year-old Irish Mary Anne Boyd of Killaghy ('formed like a Grecian nymph') seemed less of a 'belle Irlandaise' once pursued to her native shores. She was 'so young, so childish… that… I was ashamed of having raved so much about her'. Boswell even briefly considered resuming his courtship of Belle De Zuylen (see Chapter 5). However, fresh correspondence quickly gave rise to a disagreement over her proposal to translate and abridge the *Account of Corsica*. So that long-running quasi romance was finally buried. The ménage would have been like 'thunder and lightning', he concluded.

Boswell was eventually to find a true love and steady companion for a wife. But in the meantime, he indulged himself in a deliciously irregular liaison. In May of 1776, while on holiday in the rural watering place of Moffat, Boswell had met his 'dear infidel', his 'Circe', his 'Lais'. Later in the year she joined him in Edinburgh, where the house of an obliging widow served for their trysts. Now this was something: a willing, good-looking mistress; a regular, irregular diet. Boswell described her variously to a highly envious, partly censorious Temple. She was very handsome, very lively and admirably formed for amorous dalliance. She had the finest black hair; she was paradisial in bed, and so on. On the debit side, her real name was apparently Mrs Dodds (we don't know her Christian name). She was separated from her husband and three children. But Boswell explained: 'No matter. She is like a girl of eighteen.' And even if she was 'ill-bred, quite a rompish girl... Is it not right that I shall have a favourite to keep me happy?' In the spring of 1767, at least, he was enchanted with her.

All this time he was being kept busy with his new law practice. We will look at this more fully in a following chapter. However, as a son of one of the most respected Court of Session judges and (to be fair) as an able and eloquent pleader in his own right, Boswell was as busy an advocate in his first year of practice as he could reasonably have expected. In his next trip south, he was able to report to Dr Johnson that he had made £200 in the past year. The good doctor was delighted. 'He grumbled and laughed and was wonderfully pleased. "What Bozzy? Two hundred pounds! a great deal."'

In the period under discussion, Boswell generally lived at home. This was at Blair's Land in Edinburgh, during the winter and summer legal terms (mid November to mid March and mid June to mid August), and otherwise at Auchinleck. He had two trips to London: spring 1768 and autumn 1769, and a jaunt to Ireland in the early summer of that year. Thus, although the young man's life abounded with incident, there was much solid routine too.

Boswell's *Account of Corsica* was published on 18 February 1768. It was received with widespread acclaim and became swiftly popular. The book went through two official editions in just over a year, and a third was required by May 1769. The book was eventually translated into French, German and Italian. The author was suddenly famous beyond even his expectations. The reasons for the work's popularity are not hard to discern. Apart from Boswell's lively style and personal narrative, the two themes of liberty in general, and Corsica in particular, were popular topics of the moment. The American Declaration of Independence had lately been signed. The slogan, 'Wilkes and Liberty', was on everyone's lips. The excesses of the French Revolution were still some years ahead. So, for a time, the young Boswell could revel in his literary fame, enjoy his new professional status and indulge himself with his ravishing mistress. There was bound to be a reaction.

It should not be thought that Boswell's actions for the Corsican cause were purely selfish. While the island was still struggling for its independence, he attempted to put pressure on the British government to have it take decisive action in the defence of the island. He did so both directly and by way of propaganda in newspapers. However, the policy of the government was otherwise. A reply eventually obtained from Pitt, the Earl of Chatham (4 February 1767) expressed admiration for General Paoli but saw 'not the least ground at present for this country to interfere with any justice in the affairs of Corsica'. Lord Holland, Bute's political strong man, opined laconically: 'Foolish as we are, we cannot be so foolish to go to war because Mr Boswell has been in Corsica...' What this meant was that the British were to take no steps to prevent the French taking over the island. This they eventually did in the early summer of 1769. The hero chief, Paoli, apparently preferred exile to martyrdom and fled to London. Boswell was 'quite sunk' by the news. He and others had subscribed money for ordnance for the islanders, but it was too little, too late. In September of that year, at a Shakespearean Jubilee staged by Garrick at Stratford, Boswell rendered himself both conspicuous and ludicrous by appearing in a home-made Corsican chief's dress while distributing a set of hastily composed verses 'in the Character of a Corsican'. A print of him thus attired was widely distributed. He had become 'Corsica Boswell' certainly, but the tone was no longer one of admiration. Dr Johnson advised that he should 'mind his own affairs, and leave the Corsicans to theirs'.

Back in Edinburgh, the affair with Mrs Dodds was not running smoothly. Sometimes she teased James about her former lovers to such effect that he was rendered 'unfit for love'. He was frequently on the point of giving her up and would then fall gloriously back in love with her again. The incredulous Temple was advised: 'I was sometimes resolved to let her go, and sometimes my heart was like to burst within me. I held her dear hand. Her eyes were full of passion. I took her in my arms, I told her what made me miserable… we renewed our fondness. All again was well… I embraced her with transport.' The practicalities of the affair caused problems. Having persuaded his mistress that he should take a house for her, Boswell was then appalled at the expense. 'Furnishing a house and maintaining her with a maid will cost me a great deal of money, and it is too like marriage, or too much a settled plan of licentiousness. But what can I do? I have already taken the house and the lady has agreed to go into it at Whitsunday. I cannot in honour draw back. Besides, in no other way can I have her.' Moreover, he had invested the bulk of his first session's fees in house rent!

Another complication was his own behaviour. Even when busy and happy, Boswell would frequently indulge in bouts of excessive drinking. This would lead to midnight forays into the low alleys and brothels of Edinburgh, with the inevitable consequence to his health. He explained to Temple: 'My present misfortune is occasioned by drinking. Since my return to Scotland I have given a great deal too much in to that habit, which still prevails in Scotland. Perhaps the coldness of the Scots requires it. But my firey blood is turned to madness by it. This will be a warning to me, and from henceforth I shall be a perfect man. At least I hope so.' What he was referring to was a recent incident when he had dined and got very drunk with some friends. He had become

so much intoxicated that instead of going home I went to a low house in one of the alleys in Edinburgh where I knew a common girl lodged, and like a brute as I was I lay all night with her. I had still so much reason left as not to 'dive into the bottom of the deep', but I gratified my coarse desires by tumbling about on the brink of destruction. Next morning I was like a man ordered for ignominious execution. But by noon I was worse, for I discovered some infection had reached me.

He had then to go and confess all to Mrs Dodds.

Despite her forgiveness (and possibly because of his resultant incapacity), he resolved to give her up and sent her a 'firm letter' before leaving for the country. The reply took a month to come and was a shock: the lady was pregnant. Undismayed, our hero joked of the variety of his 'productions', both literary and natural. As had been the case with Peggy Doig's child (see Chapter 5), he planned to make provision for the infant.

Margaret (*Peggie*)
Montgomerie (1738 - 89).
Boswell's tolerant
and loving wife.

If it were a boy, he would call him George Keith, after the Earl Marischal. In fact, at the end of that year, 1767, Mrs Dodds presented him with Sally: 'the finest little girl I ever saw'. For a time the association was on again but, by mid 1769, Boswell was referring, in the past tense, to 'that unlucky affair'. We then hear no more of either Sally or the dark-haired Moffat enchantress.

By then, Boswell had actually fallen fully (if not finally) in love with the woman who was to be his wife. In many ways she was an unlikely candidate. She was thirty-one (two years older than Boswell), had no fortune and was not particularly good-looking. He had known her all his life, because she was his cousin, Margaret Montgomerie of Lainshaw in Ayrshire. For many years they had been the best of friends. Margaret and her family must have been frequently amused by our hero's many gallantries and courtships. She had agreed to accompany Boswell on his jaunt to Ireland in May 1769, when the young Mary Ann Boyd had been the object of the visit. Instead, and in the course of the journey, Boswell suddenly realised that all that he was looking for in a wife was by his side. He wrote to Temple (3 May 1769): 'I found her both by sea and land the best companion I ever saw. I am exceedingly in love with her. I highly value her. If ever a man had his full choice of a wife, I would have it in her.' Best of all, his feelings were reciprocated. There remained only the obstacle of Lord Auchinleck, where there was a further complication. Perhaps out of natural inclination and loneliness, perhaps out of despair of his eldest son ever amounting to anything, Lord Auchinleck had himself (at sixty-two) been harbouring thoughts of remarriage. Such a prospect was complete anathema to Boswell. He noted in his journal (16 July 1769):

> *I sent for worthy Grange, and was so furious and black-minded and uttered such horrid ideas that he could not help shedding tears, and even went so far as to say that if I talked so he would never see me again. I looked on my father's marrying again as the most ungrateful return to me for my having submitted so much to please him. I thought it an insult on the memory of my valuable mother. I thought it would totally estrange him from his children by her. In short, my wild imagination made it appear as terrible as can be conceived.*

Boswell-like, he wrote to Margaret asking if she would still marry him if they were to leave Scotland and live abroad in penury. She was to think seriously of this 'and one way or other tell me your resolution'. But Margaret had marked her man for better or for worse, and, on 25 July 1769, she wrote in reply: 'I have thought fully as you desired, and in answer to your letter I accept of your terms, and shall do everything in my power to make myself worthy of you. J.B. with £100 a year is every bit as valuable to me as if possessed of the estate of Auchinleck… '

The die was cast. As for Lord Auchinleck, he reluctantly gave his permission to the marriage but also went ahead with his own plans. On 25 November 1769, the father was married to another cousin, Elizabeth Boswell, and, apparently by design, on the same day, so were James and Margaret, at Lainshaw. On a recent visit to London, Boswell had had the marriage contract for his part witnessed by Dr Johnson and General Paoli. The local parish register noted more prosaically: 'Miss Peggie Montgomrie married'. There is no mention of the groom!

CHAPTER 7

Distinguished Visitors:

General Paoli and Dr Johnson

in Scotland

For a time after his marriage, Boswell allowed the dust to settle. He devoted himself to his legal practice and domestic affairs. His new household was first established in a modest dwelling in the Cowgate, a low-lying insalubrious part of Edinburgh. After a few months, the couple moved to better quarters in the Canongate. Then, in May 1771, they moved again to the first of two flats in James Court, which was to be their Edinburgh home for the next fifteen years. There was an early domestic set-back at the end of August 1770, when Margaret gave birth to a son who died within hours. Boswell was cast down but resilient. There would eventually be five surviving children, two sons and three daughters.

Boswell had long been keen to have his distinguished friends visit him in Scotland. His writings are full of visions of this luminary or that, strolling in the venerable glades of Auchinleck. He had broached the possibility of such a visit to Rousseau, before he became disappointed with the 'illustrious philosopher'. Voltaire, as we have seen, begged to be excused from such a visit but, given the chosen signatures on the marriage contract, it was fitting that the two celebrities who actually paid such visits were General Paoli and Dr Johnson.

Paoli, it will be recalled, had sought refuge from his native Corsica when the French defeated the partisan forces in 1769. He had since taken up residence in London as welcome guest and pensioner of the British government. He and Boswell had renewed their friendship during Boswell's visit to London in September 1769. It was presumably at that

Scenes from the Jaunt: Monboddo Castle and the Buller of Buchan:
(Original Photos by Martin Mitchell 1973).

time that an invitation to Scotland was made. In light of the considerable efforts that Boswell had exerted for the Corsican cause, the General possibly felt under some obligation to humour his supporter. In any event, with Boswell and Margaret freshly back from a holiday jaunt to the north of England, the Corsican hero, accompanied by Count Burzynkski, the Polish Ambassador, arrived 'incognito in Edinburgh on Tuesday, September 3rd [1771] at Peter Ramsay's Inn', Cowgate, Edinburgh.

The fullest version of Paoli's nine-day visit to Scotland, is found in the 'Authentick Account' written by Boswell himself for the *London Magazine*. Naturally, our subject features largely in it himself. 'The illustrious Corsican chief was all along resolved since he arrived in Great Britain to make a tour to Scotland, and visit James Boswell Esq: who was the first gentleman of this country that visited Corsica, and whose writings made the brave islanders and their General be properly known and esteemed over Europe.'

In Edinburgh, the visitors viewed the castle, Holyrood House 'and the other buildings of that City'. They visited Duddingston, the seat of Lord Abercorn, and Prestonfield, the home of Boswell's old friend, Sir Alexander Dick. On 5 September, accompanied by Boswell, 'they set out early in the morning for the west.' At Linlithgow, the travellers surveyed 'the ruins of the ancient palace of the kings of Scotland'. They admired the Forth-Clyde Canal: 'that great canal of communication between the eastern and western seas which is without question one of the greatest works in modern times'. They visited the ironworks at Carron where 'General Paoli had a peculiar pleasure in viewing the forge where were formed the cannon and warlike stores, which a Society of gentlemen in Scotland sent to the aid of the brave Corsicans'. This was truly ironic, as the 'Society', in which Boswell had played a leading part, was still due the works over £500 for the ordnance supplied! On, then, to 'the beautiful and flourishing city of Glasgow'. Soon 'the report was that General Paoli was in town and then everybody was in motion, crowding to see him.' Today, with instant media reportage of world events, it is difficult to imagine the excitement that the visit of such a foreign statesman would then have caused. In the 1770s, even an international trading metropolis like Glasgow received most of its foreign news, late and second-hand, from the London papers. Here was an international event (and its publicist) on the doorstep. Glasgow rose to the occasion. 'The streets and windows of Glasgow were quite full of spectators…' The professors of the college 'entertained their Excellencies and a number of other gentlemen of distinction with wine and sweatmeats [sic] in the Library. The Magistrates of Glasgow behaved with that dignity and propriety, which might be expected from gentlemen of extensive commerce and consequently enlarged minds. They therefore met their Excellencies at the Cross... and most politely asked the honour of their company to dinner...' It was just over eleven years before, that Boswell had found existence in the city so intolerable that he had decamped to London!

The royal progress continued to Auchinleck where the party stayed for two nights. Lord Auchinleck was reported as being 'extremely happy to receive such guests'. The following Monday, 9 September, they travelled from Glasgow to view Loch Lomond. They went up as far as Firkin Point, ascended a good way the mountains above it and had an extensive prospect of the lake both to the east and west, with Ben Lomond and other hills. At night, they came to Rossdhu, the seat of Sir James Colquhoun of Luss, where they were most hospitably entertained. Sir James's barge was ready on General Paoli's arrival, and carried him round one of the beautiful islands in Lock Lomond belonging to Sir James. In the course of this little sail, His Excellency saw the lake to great advantage and was much delighted with it. At Dumbarton, the visitors were presented with the freedom of the town and the General enjoyed the prospect of the Clyde Estuary, Greenock and Port Glasgow.

Back in Glasgow, the Lord Provost and Magistrates fulfilled their invitation. The civic dinner was held at the Saracen's Head: 'In all, 52 at table; and after dinner their Excellencies were presented with the freedom of the City, which they accepted in the politest manner.' By the afternoon of 11 September the party were back in Edinburgh where 'the General slept under the roof of his ever grateful friend.' (Boswell at his most unctuous!)

By 12 September the visit was at an end and the two distinguished guests set off again for England. 'During General Paoli's and the Ambassador's short stay at Edinburgh, they enjoyed the company of most people of distinction, learning, and genius, who are in town; and, without flourish or parade of words it may be truly said, that this visit to Scotland will be remembered in the most pleasing and honourable manner.' Among the 'people of distinction' they had met were the literati, Blair, Hume and Robertson; the physician, Dr Gregory; and the politician Henry Dundas. In contrast to Glasgow, however, Edinburgh had not honoured the visitors with either a civic reception or the freedom of the city. Boswell, of course, took this supposed affront personally. In two anonymous attacks on Lord

Provost Darlymple, published in the *London Chronicle,* he derides the Chief Magistrate as being a fat Luckenbooth merchant, who would have had nothing to say to the visitors. The fact that the Provost was a brother of his long-suffering friend and supporter, Lord Hailes, did not deter him. His Lordship was not amused.

Fortunately, by the time the next distinguished visitor was due, Lord Hailes appears to have forgiven the indiscretion. The whole Edinburgh establishment was abuzz with the news: the great Dr Johnson was to visit Scotland.

The proposed tour of the Highlands and Islands had been some years in contemplation. Boswell had first mentioned the possibility to Johnson as early as the summer of 1763. From time to time thereafter, the matter had been raised in conversation or correspondence. As the years passed, Boswell must have despaired of persuading his London-based friend (now over sixty years of age) to forsake his usual haunts and come north to the unknown. But come north he finally did, arriving at Boyd's Inn at the head of the Canongate, Edinburgh, late in the evening of Saturday, 14 August 1773.

The nature of the journey contemplated by the elderly sage and his thirty two-year-old companion might be considered somewhat risky. Twice within the last fifty years the Highlands had been in open, armed rebellion against the London government. Certainly, the draconian measures of repression and dispossession which followed the final defeat of the Jacobites in 1746 had rendered the Highlands largely safe and law-abiding. (Dr Johnson was persuaded to leave his pistols in Edinburgh). But apart from soldiers and those on government business, the only notable civilian traveller who had recently gone before was Thomas Pennant, whose valuable *Tour in Scotland* had been published in 1771. Communications had been improved by the military roads and bridges constructed by General Wade between the two Rebellions. Money from the forfeited estates of rebel land-owners had also been used for this purpose. But, once away from the principal towns, the travellers would be reduced to tracks and moorland paths, primitive ferries and Gaelic-speaking guides. Progress would be physically uncomfortable and occasionally dangerous. It would be a far cry from the pork chop and mug of ale in the Mitre Tavern.

As is well known, both Johnson and Boswell wrote accounts of the trip. The chronology of writing and publication merits attention. Dr Johnson claimed to have had the idea of writing his account while en route

Dr Johnson in his *very wide brown cloth greatcoat* while on the Highland Jaunt.

(Glenshiel, 1 September 1773):

> *I sat down on a bank, such as a writer of Romance might have delighted to feign. I had indeed no trees to whisper over my head, but a clear rivulet streamed at my feet. The day was calm, the air soft, and all was rudeness, silence and solitude. Before me, and on either side, were high hills, which by hindering the eye from ranging, forced the mind to find entertainment for itself. Whether I spent the hour well I know not; for here I first conceived the thought of this narration.*

His account, *A Journey to the Western Islands of Scotland*, was published in January 1775 to general acclaim. Boswell's own *Journal of a Tour to the Hebrides with Samuel Johnson, LL.D.* did not appear until the autumn of 1785. In fact, Boswell's journal of the tour had been written up at the time, and largely read and approved of by Dr Johnson on the journey itself. At one time, it was proposed that some of his material should be published as supplementary 'Remarks' to Dr Johnson's work, but, as it transpired, the journal was not published until after Dr Johnson's death in December 1784. Boswell clearly saw his work as a curtain-raiser to his *Life of Johnson*. There are many allusions in the *Journal* to accounts of matters to be more fully treated in the *Life*.

Since the 1920s the two accounts of their journey have been published as parallel texts. They make a fascinating contrast. Johnson's *Journey* is matter-of-fact, philosophical, magisterial in style. Boswell's *Journal* is bubbling, gossipy and full of day-to-day details. Johnson's work is largely impersonal, Boswell's is personal to the point of embarrassment. Even twelve years after the event, the publication of Boswell's book provoked mirth, outrage, caricature and threats of violence. Both works have great merit, but Boswell's is the living document.

It is not our purpose to follow minutely the footsteps of the two friends as they tramped and squelched their way over the Highlands and Islands. Many have already done so. Two of the most impressive accounts are by George Birkbeck Hill (1890) and Moray McLaren (1954). Hill was the greatest Boswell and Johnson authority of his day. His *Footsteps of Dr Johnson,* is a highly readable account of the journey and a valuable picture of the late nineteenth-century Scotland that he himself was seeing. Moray McLaren's account is an interesting and affectionate one from a Scottish viewpoint, but is prone to occasional inaccuracies, since the bulk of Boswell's journals had then still to be published in an accessible form. However, since Boswell's own *Journal* is clearly the most comprehensive of his published works to relate to Scotland, an outline of the progress of the famous journey would seem appropriate.

Boswell's purpose in persuading Johnson to visit Scotland was to have the pleasure and interest of observing the great man in an unfamiliar setting. Here Boswell could play the host and enjoy the reflected glory of his famous guest. Thus his *Journal* starts with a masterly character sketch of the doctor:

> *His person was large, robust, I may say approaching to the gigantick, and grown unwieldy from corpulency. His countenance was naturally of the cast of an ancient statue, but somewhat disfigured by the scars of that evil, which, it was formerly imagined, the royal touch could cure. He was now in his 64th year and was become a*

little dull of hearing. His sight had always been somewhat weak; yet, so much does mind govern, and even supply the deficiency of organs, that his perceptions were uncommonly quick and accurate. His head, and sometimes also his body, shook with a kind of motion like the effect of a palsy; he appeared to be frequently disturbed by cramps, or convulsive contractions, of the nature of that distemper called St Vitus's dance. He wore a full suit of plain brown clothes, with twisted hair buttons of the same colour, a large bushy greyish wig, a plain shirt, black worsted stockings and silver buckles. Upon this tour, when journeying, he wore boots, and a very wide brown cloth greatcoat, with pockets which might have almost held the two volumes of his folio dictionary; and he carried in his hand a large English oak stick. Let me not be censured for mentioning such minute particulars. Everything relative to so great a man is worth observing. I remember Dr Adam Smith, in his rhetorical lectures at Glasgow, told us that he was glad to know that Milton wore latchets in his shoes, instead of buckles.

Not satisfied with this, the author later includes a description of himself.

I have given a sketch of Dr Johnson: my readers may wish to know a little of his fellow traveller. Think then, of a gentleman of ancient blood, the pride of which was his predominant passion. He was then in his 33rd year, and had been about 4 years happily married… He had all Dr Johnson's principles, with some degree of relaxation. He had rather too little, than too much prudence; and, his imagination being lively, he often said things of which the effect was very different from the intention…

Dr Johnson was briefer and to the point:

I had desired to visit the Hebrides, or Western Islands of Scotland, so long, that I scarcely remember how the wish was originally excited; and was in the autumn of the year 1773 induced to undertake the journey, by finding in Mr Boswell a companion whose acuteness would help my enquiry, and whose gaiety of conversation and civility of manners are sufficient to counteract the inconveniences of travel, in countries less hospitable than we have passed.

A satirical view of the early part of Dr Johnson's visit by Rowlandson (1786).

Glen Moriston: a typical stretch of the Highland Countryside traversed by the travellers.

Boswell:

On Saturday the 14th of August 1773, late in the evening, I received a note from him, that he was arrived at Boyd's Inn at the head of the Canongate. I went to him directly. He embraced me cordially; and I exulted in the thought, that I now had him actually in Caledonia... He was to do me the honour to lodge under my roof... Mr Johnson and I walked arm in arm up the High Street to my house in James's Court; it was a dusky night; I could not prevent his being assailed by the evening effluvia of Edinburgh... A zealous Scotsman would have wished Mr Johnson to be without one of his five senses upon this occasion. As we marched slowly along, he grumbled in my ear, 'I smell you in the dark!' but he acknowledged that the breadth of the street, and the loftiness of the buildings on each side made a noble appearance... My wife had tea ready for him... We sat till near two in the morning having chatted a good while after my wife left us.

Distinguished contemporaries as seen by caricaturist John Kay: Lord Kames, Hugo Arnott, Lord Monboddo.

After this touching and effective account of his arrival in Edinburgh, Boswell launches into a detailed itemisation of the socialising which occupied the next three days. In contrast, by the beginning of his second paragraph, Dr Johnson has left Edinburgh ('a City too well known to admit description') and is off to the north. It was 18 August 1773, and the journey was to take eighty-three days.

The party that climbed into the boat at Leith for the crossing of the Forth to Kinghorn comprised our two travellers, Boswell's Bohemian servant, Joseph ('a fine stately fellow above six feet') and the same William Nairn who had lately engineered the escape of his niece from the Tolbooth (see Chapter 6). Dr Johnson insisted on inspecting the first curiosity en route, the rocky Isle of Inchkeith. In common with most Edinburgh residents then and now, neither of the local men had ever set foot on it. So, over the rocks they scrambled, and Dr Johnson 'stalked like a giant among the luxuriant thistles and nettles'. Not even the doctor's ironic enthusiasm for Inchkeith as a potential tourist attraction could detain the travellers long and they were soon in a post-chaise driving, via Kirkcaldy and Cupar, to arrive late at St Andrews.

Even today, when it is a thriving university and golfing town, St

Andrews retains a strong flavour of times past. Dr Johnson saw it as a former episcopal seat and university town then in decline and was depressed. The students were said not to exceed 100. The 'ruffians of reformation' had done their work to the ruined castle and cathedral. He concluded that 'the kindness of the professors did not contribute to abate the uneasy remembrance of a university declining, a college alienated, and a church profaned and hastening to the ground.' Boswell adds, more cheerfully: 'It was a very fine day… The professors entertained us with a very good dinner.'

After a day and a half spent in St Andrews the two travellers journeyed on north, via Dundee, Arbroath and Montrose to Aberdeen. Dr Johnson grumbled at the cost of ferrying the chaise over the Tay: 'Four shillings'! The ruins of the abbey at Aberbrothick, as he styled Arbroath, impressed him however. So did the agility of Boswell: 'whose inquisitiveness is seconded by great activity', as he 'scrambled in at a high window' of one of the towers 'but found the stairs within broken, and could not reach the top'. The doctor concluded: 'I should scarcely have regretted my journey, had it afforded nothing more than the sight of Aberbrothick.'

After some debate (on Boswell's part at least), the two friends decided to break their journey north from Montrose by calling on Lord Monboddo. Boswell explains: 'I knew Lord Monboddo and Dr Johnson did not love each other, yet I was unwilling not to visit His Lordship and was also curious to see them together.' Monboddo was the highly intellectual, somewhat eccentric colleague of Boswell's father, who had attracted a degree of notoriety by anticipating Darwin's ideas as to the evolution of man from the ape. This was unacceptable enough in the late eighteenth century but to maintain that the only reason mankind had no tails was that they were cropped at birth, was to invite derision. In the event, he made the two travellers very welcome. Johnson: 'The magnetism of his conversation easily drew us out of our way and the entertainment which we received would have been a sufficient recompense for a much greater deviation.' Boswell: 'His Lordship was drest in a rustic suit and wore a little round hat. He said we should have a farmers' dinner.' After some hours of chat they took leave of His Lordship and reached Aberdeen. They found the New Inn full. But, per Dr Johnson, 'Mr Boswell made himself known; his name overwhelmed all objection and we found a very good house and civil treatment.'

The travellers spent two days in Aberdeen. Dr Johnson, in his account, although fearing that a description of the city, 'as if we had been cast upon a newly discovered coast', might be thought to have 'the appearance of very frivolous ostentation', none the less provides a neat sketch of the town. 'New Aberdeen has all the bustle of prosperous trade, and all the shew of increasing oppulence. It is built by the water-side. The houses are large and lofty, and the streets spacious and clean. They build almost wholly with the granite used in the new pavements of the streets of London, which is well known not to want hardness, yet they shape it easily. It is beautiful and must be very lasting.' He also found remarkable the separate universities in New and Old Aberdeen. Boswell found it remarkable that the doctor seemed very fond of Scotch broth. Boswell: 'You never ate it before.' Johnson: 'No sir, but I don't care how soon I eat it again.' The Magistrates had decided to present their distinguished visitor (Johnson) with the freedom of the town. Boswell: 'Doctor Johnson was much pleased with this mark of attention, and received it very politely. There was a pretty numerous company assembled. It was striking to hear all of them drinking: "Doctor Johnson! Doctor Johnson!" in the Town Hall of Aberdeen, and then to see him with his Burgess-ticket, or diploma, in his hat, which he wore as he walked along the street, according to the usual custom.' Back in the comfort of their inn, the friends reflected on the distinguished citizens they had met, but concluded that the Aberdonians had not started a single mawkin (Scotch hare) for them to pursue. Generally, the Scottish intellectuals did not care to be controversial with the great doctor.

The travellers had now been six days on their journey. Dr Johnson wrote: 'The road beyond Aberdeen grew more stony and continued equally naked of all vegetable decoration.' Later, he was to observe: 'I have now travelled 200 miles in Scotland and seen only one tree not younger than myself.' Boswell did his best to point out mature woodland. Johnson, with little respect for the patriotic feelings of his hosts, insisted that all recent improvements had come from England. 'Till the Union made them acquainted with English manners, the culture of their lands was unskilful, and their domestick life unformed; their tables were coarse as the feasts of Eskimeaux, and their houses filthy as the cottages of Hottentots' (a favourite term of abuse with the doctor).

Despite such devastating observations, the doctor was enjoying his Tour. He told Boswell that he was not interested in visiting fine places, of which there were enough in England. He wanted to see 'wild objects, mountains, waterfalls, peculiar manners; in short, things which he had not seen before'. And it was Johnson who, after 'striding irregularly along' the narrow rim of the Buller of Buchan, 'insisted on taking a boat and sailing into the Pot... He was stout and wonderfully alert.'

They were still in comparatively civilised country and bowled along in their post-chaise via Banff, Elgin and Nairn to Inverness. The journey had its ups and downs. There was an inedible dinner at an inn in Elgin but an excellent one at Fort George, where the travellers were entertained by the Governor and the regimental band. Dr Johnson's imagination was stimulated by the Shakespearean implications of the route between Forres and Cawdor. Boswell: 'In the afternoon we drove over the very heath where Macbeth met the witches, according to tradition.' Dr Johnson repeated the classic lines: 'How far is't called to Fores? What are these, so wither'd, and so wild in their attire? That look not like the inhabitants o' the earth, and yet are on't?' And then, as a dig at Boswell's territorial aspirations: 'All hail Dalblair! Hail to thee, Laird of Auchinleck!'

On Saturday, 28 August, the two men reached Inverness and put up at Mackenzies Inn. As Dr Johnson put it: 'Here the appearance of life began to alter. I had seen a few women with plaids at Aberdeen; but at Inverness the Highland manners are common.' Boswell was at first discountenanced to find no letter from home, but rallied: '... I considered that I was upon an expedition for which I had wished for years, and the recollection of which would be a treasure to me for life.'

After Inverness, the travellers had to take to horse. Accompanied by two Highland guides, they travelled along Loch Ness, by Fort Augustus and Glen Shiel to Glen Elg, where they were to cross to Skye. Boswell was happy and amused to see the good doctor on horseback, 'jaunting about at his ease in quest of pleasure and novelty'. The countryside seemed wild and bleak and novelties were few. The friends diverted themselves by visiting an old woman in what would now be called a 'black house'. The structure was crude, of loose stones and heath and the interior wretched and smoke-filled. Dr Johnson, who was perhaps less used to such basic accommodation than his Scottish friend, was curious to know where the old woman slept. This gave rise to an apparently ludicrous misunderstanding, as the old lady protested to the guides in Gaelic that she feared that the travellers wanted to go to bed with her! This fear dispelled, she served the company whisky and was rewarded with a shilling and snuff. Johnson does not mention the incident of the bed, but Boswell creates a classic word picture of the travellers' merriment as they rode on.

FRONTISPIECE.

'All hail Dalblair' hail to thee Laird of Auchinleck.'

LODGING AT A M'QUEENS.

The tour in progress, according to Rowlandson.

This coquetry, or whatever it may be called, of so wretched a being, was truly ludicrous. Doctor Johnson and I afterwards were merry upon it. I said, it was he who alarmed the poor woman's virtue. 'No, sir, (said he), she'll say: "There came a wicked young fellow, a wild dog, who I believe would have ravished me, had there not been with him a grave old gentleman, who repressed him; but when he gets out of the sight of his tutor, I'll warrant you he'll spare no woman he meets, young or old."' 'No, sir, (I replied), she'll say "There was a terrible ruffian who would have forced me, had it not been for a civil decent young man who, I take it, was an angel sent from heaven to protect me."'

In truth, however, the old lady's fears might not have been quite so ridiculous as they seemed. After all, it was less than thirty years since this part of the Highlands had been subject to rape and pillage by the soldiers of the Duke of Cumberland.

By and large, the inns where the two slept had been decent enough up to this stage. Now, however, the accommodation became basic indeed. At Anoch: 'The room had some deals laid across the joists, as a kind of ceiling. There were two beds in the room, and a woman's gown was hung on a

Armadale in the early nineteenth century. One of the seats of Sir Alexander MacDonald (William Daniell, 1819).

rope to make a curtain of separation between them. Joseph had sheets, which my wife had sent with us, laid on them. We had much hesitation, whether to undress, or lie down with our clothes on. I said at last, "I'll plunge in! There will be less harbour for vermin about me, when I am stripped!"' At Glen Elg, things were even worse. Boswell reported: 'A maid showed us upstairs into a room, damp and dirty, with bare walls, a variety of bad smells, a coarse black greasy fir table, and forms of the same kind; and out of a wretched bed started a fellow from his sleep," described by Dr Johnson as 'a man black as a Cyclops from the forge'. The doctor slept on hay in his riding coat. 'Mr Boswell, being more delicate, laid himself sheets with hay over and under him, and lay in linen like a gentleman.'

As they approached Glen Elg and the sea, the travellers had what amounted to the most serious quarrel of the journey. Boswell, anxious to arrange accommodation and a boat for the passage to Skye, had made to ride on ahead. Dr Johnson, for all his fortitude of character, suddenly alarmed at the prospect of being left alone in the wilderness with the servants, 'called me back with a tremendous shout and was really in a passion at me for leaving him'. Even later, 'He was still violent upon that head, and said, "Sir, had you gone on, I was thinking that I should have returned with you to Edinburgh, and then have parted from you, and

The house of Talisker, Skye (in 1973): Dr Johnson compared the mountain in the background to a haystack.

never spoken to you more.'" In the morning, the doctor was repentant and all was well again: 'Let's think no more on't.'

It was after breakfast on Thursday, 2 September 1773, that Johnson and Boswell took a boat across to Skye. They were to spend almost two months in the islands of the Inner Hebrides. Part of this time was involuntary. September can be a fine month in Scotland but it was not to be so for our travellers. Time and time again they were storm-bound by violent weather. On one occasion, they were in real danger of their lives.

Initially, however, all was optimism. Their first host was to be Sir Alexander MacDonald, whose ancestors had been the Lords of the Isles. By coincidence, he had married a distant Yorkshire cousin of Boswell, once considered by the latter as one of his many matrimonial prospects. The visit, then, should have been a happy one. Alas it was not to be so. Sir Alexander and his lady were staying at Armadale, one of their smaller properties, as they were en route to Edinburgh. Because of the circumstances and, it appears, the natural parsimony of their host, the two travellers were not treated with the kind of hospitality that they clearly expected. Boswell (in the first edition of the *Journal* at least) had some harsh things to say about this.

*Instead of finding the head of the MacDonalds surrounded with his
clan, and a festive entertainment, we had a small company, and
cannot boast of our cheer. The particulars are minuted in my
'Journal' but I shall not trouble the public with them. I shall mention
but one characteristic circumstance. My shrewd and hearty friend,
Sir Thomas Blacket, Lady MacDonald's uncle, who had preceded us
in a visit to this Chief, upon being asked by him, if the punch-bowl
then upon the table was not a very handsome one, replied 'Yes – if it
were full.'… I meditated an escape from this house the very next day;
but Doctor Johnson resolved that we should weather it out till
Monday.*

When Boswell's account came out in 1785, even although it was twelve
years after the event, Sir Alexander was furious at these aspersions. He
sent Boswell a violent and abusive letter. The subsequent exchanges
almost led to a duel but the matter was compromised by Boswell agreeing
to omit some passages and soften others. Enough still remained, however,
to give the reading public the flavour of what must have been a less than
successful visit.

Fortunately, the next main port of call, the Isle of Raasay, proved a
delight. Boswell: 'It was past six o'clock when we arrived. Some excellent
brandy was served round immediately, according to the custom of the
Highlands, where a dram is generally taken every day… Soon afterwards a
fiddler appeared, and a little ball began. Raasay himself danced with as
much spirit as any man and Malcolm bounded like a roe.' Johnson: 'Our
reception exceeded our expectations. We found nothing but civility,
elegance and plenty. After the usual refreshments and the usual
conversation, the evening came upon us. The carpet was then rolled off
the floor; the musician was called and the whole company was invited to
dance, nor did ever fairies trip with greater alacrity.' Here, then, as at many
of the other places visited, the two guests were entertained by Highland
music and singing. In Mull, the physician's daughter even played to them
on a spinnet 'which, though made so long ago as 1667, was still very well
toned'. Dr Johnson was very impressed: 'She is the most accomplished
lady I have found in the Highlands.'

Whatever the company, Boswell was anxious to instigate and record the
doctor's table talk. He said of himself:

*I also may be allowed to claim some merit in leading the conversation:
I do not mean leading, as in an orchestra, by playing the first fiddle; but*

leading as one does in examining a witness – starting topics, and making him pursue them. He appears to me like a great mill, into which a subject is thrown to be ground. It requires, indeed, fertile minds to furnish materials for this mill. I regret whenever I see it unemployed; but sometimes I feel myself quite barren, and having nothing to throw in.

Despite this constant prompting, the doctor remained largely good-humoured, apart from the occasion when, in desperation perhaps, Boswell asked him if he had ever worn a nightcap! Then, confessed the journaliser, did he feel himself come within 'the whiff and wind of his fell sword'. He observed wryly elsewhere that the sage was most unwilling to be worsted in argument; if he missed with his pistol shot, he would bludgeon his opponent with the butt.

En route to Dunvegan, in the west of Skye, the travellers stayed at Kingsburgh, the home of the celebrated heroine of the '45, Flora Macdonald. Johnson was given the very bed which had been occupied by Charles Edward Stuart, the royal fugitive. Boswell was highly amused at his arch-Tory friend so accommodated. 'To see Doctor Samuel Johnson lying in that bed, in the Isle of Skye, in the house of Miss Flora Macdonald, struck me with such a group of ideas as it is not easy for words to describe,

Dunvegan Castle as it was in 1789: from Francis Grose's *Antiquities of Scotland*.

The stormy voyage between Skye and Coll as seen by Rowlandson. Boswell desperately holding his rope!

as they passed through the mind. He smiled, and said, "I have had no ambitious thoughts in it."' Boswell then takes the opportunity, in his book, to expand upon the various accounts of the Prince's escape that he had heard while in Skye.

Dunvegan is the ancestral home of the Macleods. After a difficult ride over boggy country, the travellers arrived late in the afternoon.

> *Boswell: The great size of the castle, which is partly old and partly new, and is built upon a rock close to the sea, while the land around it presents nothing but wild, moorish, hilly, and craggy appearances, gave rude magnificence to the scene. Having dismounted, we ascended a flight of steps, which was made by the late Macleod for the accommodation of persons coming to him by land, there formerly being, for security, no other access to the castle but from the sea… We were introduced into a stately dining room and received by Lady Macleod… Our entertainment here was in so elegant a style, and reminded my fellow traveller so much of England, that he became quite joyous. He laughed and said, 'Boswell, we came in at the wrong end of this island' – 'Sir, (said I), it was best to keep this for the last' – He answered, 'I would have it both first and last.'*

So the doctor would fain have stayed on beyond the few days allotted, but by now it was late September and the weather was deteriorating.

The party then travelled south in Skye with a view to sailing over the Sound to Mull. For days on end, the weather was against them. The doctor grew fretful. At last, on Sunday, 3 October, the travellers were told that the wind was fair for the voyage. By great good fortune, the young Laird of Coll had become one of their travelling companions. If it had not been for his fortitude and presence of mind, the journey might well have had a tragic outcome. As the boat sailed on towards Ardnamurchan Point, the weather worsened. Dr Johnson took himself below deck. Boswell remained above, first fascinated, then terrified by the ensuing scene. It gave rise to one of his best descriptive passages:

When we got in full view of the Point of Ardnamurchan, the wind changed, and was directly against our getting into the Sound. We were then obliged to tack, and get forward in that tedious manner. As we advanced, the storm grew greater, and the sea very rough. Coll then began to talk of making for Egg, or Canna, or his own island. Our skipper said he would get us into the Sound. Having struggled for this a good while in vain, he said he would push forward till we were near the land of Mull, where we might cast anchor and lie till the morning... Our crew consisted of one Macdonald, our skipper, and two sailors, one of whom had but one eye... The scheme of running for Canna seemed then to be embraced; but Canna was ten leagues off, all out of our way; and they were afraid to attempt the harbour of Egg. All these different plans were successively in agitation... At last it became so rough, and threatened to be so much worse, that Coll and his servant took more courage and said they would undertake to hit one of the harbours in Coll. 'Then let us run for it in God's name,' said the skipper; and instantly we turned towards it... I was relieved when I found we were to run for the harbour before the wind. But my relief was but of short duration; for I soon heard that our sails were very bad and were in danger of being torn in pieces, in which case we should be driven upon the rocky shore of Coll. It was very dark and there was a heavy and incessant rain... Our vessel often lay so much on one side that I trembled lest she should be overset... I now saw what I never saw before, a prodigious sea, with immense billows coming upon a vessel, so as that it seemed hardly possible to escape. There was something grandly horrible in the sight. I am glad I have seen it once... As I saw them all busy doing something, I asked Coll, with much earnestness, what I could do. He, with a happy readiness put into my hand a rope, which was fixed to the top of one of the masts, and told me to hold it till be bade me pull. If I had considered the matter, I might have seen that this could not be of the least service; but his object was to keep me out of the way of those who were busy working the vessel, and at the same time to divert my fear by employing me, and make me think that I was of use. Thus did I stand firm to my post, while the wind and rain beat upon me, always expecting a call to pull my rope… At last they spied the harbour of Lochiern, and Coll cried, 'Thank God, we are safe'… Doctor Johnson had all this time been quiet and unconcerned. He had lain down on one of the beds, and having got free from sickness, was satisfied… He was lying in philosophick tranquillity, with a greyhound of Coll's at his back, keeping him warm.

A few days were spent recuperating in Coll, waiting for the weather to permit their onward travels. By 14 October, they had reached Tobermory. This was almost civilisation: 'After having been shut up so long in Coll, the sight of such an assemblage of moving habitations, containing such a variety of people, engaged in different pursuits, gave me much gaiety of spirit. When we had landed, Doctor Johnson said, "Boswell is now all alive… He gets new vigour whenever he touches the ground."' There remained only Inchkenneth and Iona to visit. The visit to Iona gave rise to one of the more memorable passages in Dr Johnson's *Journey:*

We were now treading that illustrious Island, which was once the luminary of the Caledonian regions, whence savage clans and roving barbarians derived the benefits of knowledge, and the blessings of religion… Far from me and from my friends, be such frigid philosophy as may conduct us indifferent, and unmoved over any ground which has been dignified by wisdom, bravery, or virtue. That man is little to be envied, whose patriotism would not gain force upon the plain of Marathon, or whose piety would not grow warmer among the ruins of Iona!

On a less lofty note, Boswell records that, despite having the Chief of the McLean clan with them, the best accommodation which could be offered was a large barn. 'Some good hay was strewed at one end of it, to form a bed for us, upon which we lay with our clothes on; and we were furnished with blankets from the village. Each of us had a portmanteau for a pillow. When I awakened in the morning, and looked around me, I could not help smiling at the idea of the Chief of the McLeans, the great English Moralist, and myself, lying thus extended in such a situation.'

The last night in Mull was spent at Moy, the seat of the Laird of Lochbuie. Although reputed to be something between a Falstaff and Don Quixote, the laird proved to be 'only a bluff, comely, noisy old gentleman, proud of his hereditary consequence, and a very hearty and hospitable landlord... Being told that Doctor Johnson did not hear well, Lochbuie bawled out to him, "Are you of the Johnstons of Glen Cro, or of Ardnamurchan?" Doctor Johnson gave him a significant look, but made no answer; and I told Lochbuie that he was not Johnston, but Johnson, and that he was an Englishman.'

At last, on 22 October, the couple

bade adieu to Lochbuie, and to our very kind conductor Sir Allan McLean, on the shore of Mull, and then got into the ferry-boat, the bottom of which was strewed with branches of trees or bushes, upon which we sat. We had a good day and a fine passage, and in the evening landed at Oban, where we found a tolerable inn. After having been so long confined at different times in islands, from which it was always uncertain when we could get away, it was comfortable to be now on the mainland, and to know that, if in health, we might get to any place in Scotland or England in a certain number of days [Boswell].

Thus was the island jaunting complete. But the way overland to Inveraray was to prove almost as arduous. Dr Johnson:

On the next day we began our journey southwards. The weather was tempestuous. For half the day the ground was rough, and our horses were still small... In the latter part of the day, we came to a firm and smooth road made by the soldiers on which we travelled with great security, busied with contemplating the scene about us. The night came on while we had yet a great part of the way to go, though not so dark, but that we could discern the cataracts which poured down the hills, on one side, and fell into one general channel that ran with great violence on the other. The wind was loud, the rain was heavy,

and the whistling of the blast, the fall of the shower, the rush of the cataracts and roar of the torrent, made a nobler chorus of the rough musick of nature than it had ever been my chance to hear before...
At last we came to Inveraray, where we found an inn not only commodious, but magnificent.

This was rare praise from the doctor for a Scottish establishment, perhaps enhanced in memory by the good supper and the gill of whisky which the two shared. '"Come", said he [Johnson], "let me know what it is that makes a Scotsman happy"!'

But Inveraray posed a dilemma. It was, of course, the seat of the Duke of Argyll, and a call on His Grace would clearly be in order. However, the Duchess was formerly the Duchess of Hamilton and thus the arch-enemy to the Douglas faction of which Boswell had been chief propagandist (see Chapter 6). The doctor was consulted and felt that Boswell at least should pay his respects. If they were formally invited, well and good. As for the Duchess: 'That, sir [the Duke] must settle with his wife.' A call on the Duke after dinner secured the invitation. It also ensured Boswell a cool reception from Her Grace. At dinner the next night, the Duchess made much of Johnson while stolidly ignoring Boswell. The latter, not to be outdone, decided to have 'the satisfaction for once to look the Duchess in the face with a glass in my hand'. He rose and proposed her health. Later, the redoubtable Duchess got her own back when the question of the Highland belief in the second sight came up. Boswell: 'I made some remark that seemed to imply a belief in second sight. The Duchess said, "I fancy you will be a Methodist." This was the only sentence Her Grace deigned to utter to me; and I take it for granted, she thought it a good hit on my credulity in the Douglas cause.'

With Dr Johnson mounted, 'like a bishop... on a stately steed from His Grace's stable', the little party then rode on via Glencoe, 'a black and dreary region' (Johnson) to Rossdhu on Loch Lomond-side. By 28 October, the travellers had arrived at the Saracens Head Inn in Glasgow, and the Highlands were behind them.

Johnson was impressed by Glasgow. 'The prosperity of its commerce appears by the greatness of many private houses, and a general appearance of wealth.' Boswell took the opportunity to repay a jibe at the Scots. Once, in London, Adam Smith (Boswell's old professor) had been boasting of Glasgow's improvement. Dr Johnson had asked him, ironically: 'Pray, sir, have you ever seen Brentford?' So, while the professors showed

Boswell's untypical reserve on the famous quarrel between Lord Auchinleck and Dr Johnson, was not shared by Rowlandson!

them round the city and the guest was expressing his admiration, Boswell whispered: 'Don't you feel some remorse?'

Coming down into Ayrshire, on 30 October they visited the Earl of Loudoun who 'jumped with joy' to see them, and met the ninety-five-year-old dowager countess who (as Johnson wrote to Mrs Thrale) sent her seventy-years-old daughter 'after supper early to bed, for girls must not use late hours'. On 1 November they surveyed 'the castle of Dundonald, which was one of the many residences of the kings of Scotland, and in which Robert the Second lived and died. Dr Johnson, to irritate my old Scottish enthusiasm, was very jocular on the homely accommodation of "King Bob", and roared and laughed till the ruins echoed.' They were on their way to Auchans where lived the dowager Countess of Eglinton, another old lady who enchanted Johnson.

The two friends were now due to spend a day or two at Auchinleck. This was a part of the journey that had caused Boswell some apprehension. Both his friend and his father were of strong, overbearing temperaments. Both were opinionated and did not care to be contradicted. 'He was as sanguine a Whig and Presbyterian as Doctor Johnson was a Tory and Church of England man. Surely the sparks would fly. Knowing all this, I should not have ventured to bring them together, had not my father, out of kindness to me, desired me to invite Doctor Johnson to his house.'

At first all went well. It was very rainy but there was Lord Auchinleck's splendid library to amuse the guest. In the dry intervals, the doctor clambered with Boswell among the ruins of the old castle, affording 'striking images of ancient life'. The inevitable explosion came late in the week. Boswell:

> *If I recollect right, the contest began while my father was shewing him his collection of medals; and Oliver Cromwell's coin unfortunately introduced Charles I and Toryism. They became exceedingly warm, and violent, and I was very much distressed by being present at such an altercation between two men, both of whom I reverenced; yet I durst not interfere. It would certainly be very unbecoming in me to exhibit my honoured father, and my respected friend, as intellectual gladiators, for the entertainment of the publick...*

But, of course, the public were entertained and Rowlandson made it his business to record the quarrel in one of his *Picturesque Beauties of Boswell*. At least Lord Auchinleck appears to have escaped the full force of Johnsonian wrath, which was reserved for Boswell's old tutor, the Rev John Dun, now the parish minister. He had the temerity to cast aspersions on the Church of England. 'He talked before Doctor Johnson, of fat bishops and drowsy deans... Sir, retorted Johnson "you know no more of our Church than a Hottentot" – I was sorry that he brought this upon himself.'

The travellers set off for Edinburgh on 8 November and, after an overnight stop at Hamilton, they arrived in the capital. Boswell... 'We arrived this night at Edinburgh, after an absence of eighty three days. For five weeks together, of the tempestuous season, there had been no account received of us. I cannot express how happy I was on finding myself again at home.'

Twelve days remained of the visit. They were passed in calls to and by the illustrious and curious. A notable exception from the guest list was David Hume, a good friend of Boswell and already famous as philosopher and historian. The reason is obvious enough: Hume had a reputation as a deist, atheist and sceptic. Johnson, as we know, was highly orthodox in his faith. A meeting would have been disastrous. As it was, Boswell recorded in his 'private' journal that the doctor had snorted: 'I know not indeed whether he has first been a blockhead and that has made him a rogue, or first been a rogue and that has made him a blockhead.' So, two of the greatest thinkers of their age were not to meet.

Boswell records the end of the visit thus: 'My illustrious friend, being now desirous to be again in the great theatre of life and animated exertion, took a place in the coach, which was to set out for London on Monday 22nd November.' In fact, he accompanied his friend, via Hawthornden and Cranston, as far as the inn at Blackshiels, before 'the coach came and took him up'. He concludes:

> I have now completed my account of our tour to The Hebrides. I have brought Doctor Johnson down to Scotland, and seen him into the coach which in a few hours carried him back into England. He said to me often, that the time he spent in this Tour was the pleasantest part of his life, and asked me if I would lose the recollection of it for £500. I answered I would not; and he applauded my setting such a value on an accession of new images in my mind.

Then, the inevitable puff for himself: 'Had it not been for me, I am persuaded Doctor Johnson would never have undertaken such a journey; and I must be allowed to assume some merit from having been the cause that our language has been enriched with such a book as that which he published on his return...'

Dr Johnson, for his part, ends his account with a visit to Mr Braidwood's 'College for the Deaf and Dumb' in Edinburgh. Tongue in cheek, he concludes: '. . . after having seen the deaf taught arithmetick, who would be afraid to cultivate the Hebrides?'

All in all, then, the visit and journey had been a great success. And, when one bears in mind that not just one, but two, classic travel books have been the direct result, perhaps Boswell can be excused for patting his own back.

CHAPTER 8

The Middle Years:
1770-1782

The middle years of a professional man's life should ideally be ones of consolidation and attainment. In Boswell's case, this should have meant professional advancement and private happiness. That there were periods of the latter will be seen, but, at the end of the period under review, the forty-year-old Boswell was apprehensive of his future as an advocate and still without any paid office. He was increasingly despondent about daily life in Scotland and about the state of his wife's health. His literary output had been confined to essays and pamphlets. He was torn and undecided as to whether Edinburgh or London should be his normal home. Relations between himself and his father and with the second Lady Auchinleck had remained strained over the years. His finances were not good. Yet at the start of the 1770s all had seemed set fair for success. He was a rising young advocate, well-known son of a famous father. He was a happily married man, proud father of a young family. He was the friend of the famous. So where and how had everything gone wrong?

The answer, of course, lay in Boswell's own personality. One day he could be the best company in the world, the next so low that he could only snarl at his wife and family. He was chronically uncertain as to the future course his life should take. In March 1780, he noted in his journal:

> *I was sensible that a great deal of the coarse law in Scotland would hurt my mind; and I should have considered that one of my fortune would be satisfied with little practice. I however dreaded*

insignificance, while at the same time I had all this year as yet been
so averse to the business of the Court of Session that I had no
keenness for it, as I once had, and wished always to have anything I
had to do, decently over. I saw no opportunity for ambition in this
narrow sphere . . . Fain would I have indulged gay, animating hopes
of exerting myself in London... Then I considered that the expensive
living in London would impoverish me, and that I might perhaps in
my hypochondriac discontent wish for the 'home' in Edinburgh. I
was sick-minded today. The Session rose, which was rather
dispiriting to me, as I was not to go to London and would mould in
inactivity.

And yet the 1770s had seen triumphs, both professional and literary. He had experienced long periods of 'felicity' and 'bliss'. He was, periodically at least, as in love with his wife as when he had married her. Their growing family was a consistent source of pleasure. Dr Johnson remained a staunch ally, and at long, long last (at the end of August 1782), he became the Laird of Auchinleck.

Boswell's preferred pattern of life over these years was to be in Edinburgh for the winter session of the court (November to March), to spend three months or so in London, return to Edinburgh for the summer session (June to August) and to spend some time in the autumn with his father at Auchinleck.

London remained the magnet. Here was the resort of the great, the gay, the magnificent, the ingenious. Here, Boswell could shine. Of his visit in the spring of 1778, for example, he wrote:

I deposited my baggage and hastened to Dr Johnson's. I was resolved
to maintain a calm mastery of myself this time in London, and not
to grow giddy in it as usual. I resolved to take London as one takes
mercury; to intermit the use of it whenever I should feel it affect my
brain... I was struck with agreeable wonder and admiration by
contemplating the immensity of the metropolis and the multitude of
objects; above all, by the number and variety of people; and all
melancholy was as clearly dissipated as if it had never existed in my
mind.

Boswell visited London eight times between 1772 and 1781. The journey, normally via Newcastle, York, Doncaster and Grantham, would take about

The Social round atVauxhall Gardens, London, c.1784, as viewed by Rowlandson. Boswell and Johnson supping to the left?

five days. '19th March 1772: We arrived in London about five o'clock, having taken just about five days to the journey, and indeed it cannot be performed in less with comfort; that is to say, taking a moderate degree of refreshments of eating, drinking and sleeping, which one ought surely to do unless when some necessity obliges one to hurry.' Sometimes the stages would leave in the early hours of the morning. They were frequently cold and uncomfortable. But Boswell was a resilient and cheerful traveller. He took pleasure in the peculiarities of his travelling companions and, when in the mood, would drew them out with his own pleasing conversation.

> *Friday, 2nd April 1773: There came into the fly this morning Mr —,*
> *who had been a strolling player, and Master ——, a young*
> *gentleman at Grantham school who was going to London to see his*
> *father and mother during the holidays. The former soon opened, and*
> *told me he had been bred a coach-painter in Long Acre, London. But*

having always a violent inclination for the stage, he went upon it, as he said, with design to be cured of his fondness for it. He had now given it up, and was to settle in business as a grocer. He lived near Biggleswade, and told me that he had many Roman coins found in that neighbourhood. He promised to send me some to Donaldson's shop in London... I do maintain that for a man in good health who just wants to be conveyed from Edinburgh to London, the fly is an excellent method; better than going with a companion in a post-chaise, such as chance supplies.

The London Journals are mainly concerned with the social round that Boswell plunged into. Calls were paid and received. Dinners taken and given. Many nights full of brilliant conversation and hard drinking. In the earlier years, much whoring and resolution to do better.

But there was also a serious side. There was some professional business. On the 1772 visit, he appeared before the House of Lords, sitting as the final court of appeal, in the case of Hastie, schoolmaster at Campbeltown, who had been dismissed because of severity to his pupils. This was a strange concept in the eighteenth century when brutal beatings were part and parcel of most boys' education. Boswell to Johnson: 'To speak candidly, sir, this man was rather too severe.' Johnson: 'Has he broke any bones?' Boswell: 'No.' Johnson: 'Has he fractured any skulls?' Boswell: 'No.' Johnson: 'Then, sir, he is safe enough. My master at Lichfield, Hunter, used to beat us unmercifully. He erred in not making a distinction between mistake and negligence; for he would beat a boy equally for not knowing a thing as for neglecting to know it.' Fortunately, their Lordships disagreed and the schoolmaster's dismissal was upheld. Boswell describes his appearance before them (14 April 1772) thus:

I was in a flutter till it was my turn to speak. When Lord Mansfield called out, 'Mr Boswell', and I mounted the little elevation on which the Counsel who speaks is placed, I felt much palpitation. But I knew I was master of my cause, and had my speech in writing. I had seen that Lord Mansfield was against us, which was discouraging. My client was now no longer at stake. I had only my own reputation to mind. I began with a very low voice and rose gradually; but restrained myself from appearing anyhow bolder even easy. I spoke slowly and distinctly, and, as I was told afterwards, very well...

William Murray, First Earl
of Mansfield (1705 - 93):
*He chills the most
generous blood* - Boswell.
Portrait by Copley *(1783)*.

Lord Mansfield, Chief Justice of the King's Bench, was a Scotsman, and one of the leading lawyers of the eighteenth century. Boswell met him socially but with qualified success. 'My Lord and I were then left tête-à-tête. His cold reserve and sharpness, too, were still too much for me. It was like being cut with a very, very cold instrument. I had not for a long time experienced that weakness of mind which I had formerly in a woeful degree in the company of the great or the clever but Lord Mansfield had uncommon power. He chills the most generous blood.' Moreover, His Lordship did not think that Scots counsel should flock to the English Bar. 'He has not the education for it. A man of very extraordinary parts may perhaps succeed.'

There were also less interesting cases to appear in, usually concerning disputed Scots election results. Indeed, Boswell noted that the expenses of his 1775 visit to London were largely covered by fees earned.

Another serious professional concern was to seek some salaried

Edmund Burke (1729 - 97):
Statesman and Orator.
He thought Boswell should
stay in Edinburgh.

government position. Boswell's chief hope in this connection was Lord
Mountstuart, the son of Lord Bute, and Boswell's old touring companion in
Italy (see Chapter 5). The nobleman blew hot and cold. He was sure that a
Court of Session gown could be obtained for Boswell in due course. Lord
Auchinleck was more realistic and reminded Boswell that the only patron
he had in fact found was himself.

Although his father would not have thought so, the other serious motive
behind the London visits was the furtherance of Boswell's literary career.
Largely through his friendship with Dr Johnson, Boswell had, over the
years, met and become friendly with the bulk of the London literary and
artistic establishment: David Garrick, Sir Joshua Reynolds, Oliver
Goldsmith, Edmund Burke, and two more personal friends, Bennet
Langton and Topham Beauclerk.

Dr Johnson and the others were members of an exclusive literary club,
known simply as 'The Club'. This met each week during the Parliamentary
terms at a selected tavern. There, over port and claret, the literary and
artistic issues of the day were discussed and praise or ridicule poured
upon current productions. Boswell was very keen to be a member of this
exclusive and influential circle. Dr Johnson was persuaded and, on 23

April 1773, proposed his friend as a member. The all-important meeting was the next week. Boswell was left at Topham Beauclerk's in the company of the latter's wife (incidentally, the Lady Diana Spencer of *her* day) while the others voted on his admission. He noted:

> *The gentlemen went away to their Club, and as one black ball could exclude, I sat in such anxious suspense as even the charms of Lady Diana Beauclerk's conversation could hardly relieve. Mr Beauclerk's coach returned for me in less than an hour with a note from him that I was chosen… I hastened to the Turks Head in Gerard Street, Soho, and was introduced to such a society as can seldom be found… Upon my entrance, Johnson… placed himself behind a chair on which he leant as on a desk or pulpit, and with humorous formality gave me a charge, pointing out the duties incumbent upon me as a good member of the Club.*

There was no doubt that Boswell owed his admission to the respect which the other members had for Dr Johnson. As the doctor put it: 'they knew that if they refused you, they'd probably never have got in another. I'd have kept them all out.'

Sometimes Boswell's activities in London were not so respectable. From time to time he indulged himself in the grossest of sensuality. In an extraordinary episode (even by his standards) over a period of only four days, at the end of March 1776, he lies with a 'strumpet' at the entry to the passage from Hay Hall, by Lord Shelbourne's, 'awakes, ill with sickness and headache', 'fears having caught the "venereal disorder", goes to look for the girl to check her health, fails to find her, but returning to the park about 3 o'clock,' observes 'a pretty, fresh looking girl', who tells him that she is a serving maid 'out on an errand', takes *her* to a house of lewd entertainment and enjoys her. But next day, after 'high Mass in the Bavarian Chapel', he dines in good company and

> *when I got out into the street the whoring rage came upon me. I thought I would devote a night to it. I was weary at the same time that I was tumultuous. I went to Charing Cross Bagnio with a wholesome looking, bouncing wench, stripped and went to bed with her. But after my desires were satiated by repeated indulgence, I could not rest; so I parted from her after she had honestly delivered my watch and ring and handkerchief, which I should not have*

missed I was so drunk. I took a hackney-coach and was set down in
Berkeley Square, and went home, cold and disturbed and dreary
and vexed, with remorse rising like a black cloud...

And if that was not enough, the very next day:

I went to Duck Lane, Westminster, and found my last night's harlot,
by the name of Nanny Cooms, and persuaded myself that she was
not infected. But whom did I see in that blackguard lane but my
pretended servant maid, Nanny Smith, in a drummers coat by way
of a morning jacket! I was abashed and mortified at my simplicity. I
asked Nanny Cooms and a girl who was with her about that jade
Smith. She said she had lived in the house with them three months,
and they could not answer for her, for the young man who lived with
her, a corporal, was now in the hospital. This made me almost sick
with fear, but Nanny Cooms had last night spoken to me of a pretty
fair girl who was on call. I sent for her and enjoyed her...

Naturally, this kind of restless activity probably cost our hero dear, not least in terms of his health. Frequently, when he returned to Edinburgh, he was accompanied by 'Signor Gonorrhoea'.

In this, and many other regards, his wife was a saint. Her health would not permit her to be in London with her husband, but the after-effects of his 'riot' would be all too plain. In addition, Boswell was a compulsive confessor. On one occasion, his physician friend Sir John Pringle advised him to sin once more, by *not* telling his wife what he had been up to.

After these social and sensual whirls, it is little wonder that the resumption of the Edinburgh round seemed dull and depressing. Particularly as the years go on, we find Boswell increasingly prone to boredom and melancholy. Towards the end of the 1770s he was sometimes so ill with the after-effects of a night's debauch, or simply so debilitated with depression, that he was unable to rise to see to his business in the Court of Session.

But, at the start of the 1770s, Boswell was, like every other young advocate, keen to take cases and win them. Thanks to his journals and other records, we know a great deal about his professional career. There is his 'Consultation Book', running from the day of his call in July 1766 to the end of the summer session of 1772. In this, he records his cases and the fees received. He frequently notes his earnings in a year or session.

The first page of Boswell's fee book, recording his early cases.
The book runs on to 1772.

Typically he would receive two or four guineas for a case and could total about 300 guineas in a full year. If a factor of about 100 is placed on these figures, a rough idea of the level of his earnings at 1970s values can be obtained. He was what would be termed in the profession today a 'middle

Parliament House, Edinburgh in the late eighteenth century (from Arnot's *History of Edinburgh*, 1779)

earner'. Top counsel like Islay Campbell (a future Lord President of the Court) and Robert McQueen, Lord Braxfield to be, could earn more than 1,500 guineas in a good year: Dr Johnson: 'Then what remains for the rest of the nation?' But with a supplementary annual allowance of £300 from his father, Boswell was comfortable enough. Twenty years later, Sir Walter Scott was not to do so well. He is said never to have earned more than £230 in any one year at the Bar. But Scott, it must be said, had much more success than Boswell in achieving salaried office, both as Sheriff (£300) and then as a Principal Clerk to the Court (£800).

Through Boswell's pen we have a unique and valuable insight into life at the Scottish Bar in the 1770s. The Faculty of Advocates was small, consisting of something over 100 practising members. The strengths, weaknesses and foibles of each member would be known to all. There was not the same remoteness between advocate and judge as existed in England. The norm was to litigate by day and socialise by night. Boswell and his friends were the wits of the Scottish professional scene. He writes typically of the start of a legal term in the summer of 1774: 'The Court of Session seemed to be crowded. I said "There must be carrion in the wind

The Upper and Laigh Parliament Halls, as they are today.

when there are so many of us." The President was ill... I was in good
sound hearty spirits, and found many of my brethren at the bar in the same
humour. The Outer House was a scene of unbounded conversation and
merriment. Everything is thrown out, and amongst such a quantity of stuff
some good things cast up...'

Boswell himself described daily procedures in the Court of Session in a letter to his friend Temple, written in February 1767, shortly after his call.

You know, one half of the business before the Court of Session is carried on by writing. In the first instance, the cause is pleaded through the Lord Ordinary, that is to say one of the fifteen judges who sits in his turn for a week in the Outer House. But no sooner does he give judgement than we give him in representations and answers and replies and duplies and triplies, and he will sometimes order memorials to give him a full view of the cause. Then we reclaim to the Inner House by petition, and there again we give in a variety of printed papers, from which the Lords determine the cause. For it is only in causes of great consequence that the Court orders a hearing in presence. This method of procedure is admirable, for it gives the judges a complete state of every question, and by binding up the session papers a man may lay up a treasure of law reasoning and a collection of extraordinary facts.

Much of the work was thus in writing. Boswell's clerk, John Lawrie, would come to him early in the morning before the court sat at nine a.m., to take dictation. 'I have dictated forty folio pages to him in one day,' Boswell reported proudly to Temple. On one less meritorious occasion, in December 1776, the author reports: 'We dined, but did not drink very much. I, however, could not resist cards... and I played at brag till near twelve. Mr Lawrie came for me, it being the last night for representing in a cause. I actually dictated a paper of four pages as I played at brag...'

Then, as now, the reputation of an advocate was made by his eloquence. There can be no doubt that Boswell was an accomplished speaker. His performance before the House of Lords in Hastie's case was praised by David Garrick, the leading actor of his day. But, eloquent or not, discretion was never a strong point with Boswell. On one occasion (March 1781), when he thought that the Lord President of the Court was impugning the political independence of the pleaders before him (as he was), he protested volubly and 'craved the protection of the Court. Some of the Lords shook their heads to make me quiet, and some about me also composed me; and so it rested.' This sort of incident, taken with a long-standing coolness between Boswell and the powerful Dundas family, was not helpful when questions of preferment arose.

Advocates by John Kay (1810):
then as now!

The criminal trial of John Reid, an alleged sheep stealer (August 1774), in which Boswell was for the defence, is the case most commonly commented upon in reviewing Boswell's early legal career. There are various reasons for this: the issues are easy to understand; the setting, involving a man on trial for his life, is dramatic; and Boswell himself has left an uncommonly detailed account of the trial and its aftermath. It should be recalled, however, that this was a trial of little moment in the general scheme of things. It earned the pleader no fee and it is difficult to maintain that an injustice was done, as Reid had been narrowly acquitted on a similar matter in 1766. What is extraordinary, and also useful in illustrating Boswell's personality, is the aftermath. First, Boswell seriously contemplated the recovery of his hanged client and engaging a surgeon to try and revive him. The dangers of involving himself in a charge of attempting to pervert the course of justice do not appear to have occurred to him. Abandoning this folly, he then petitioned for a royal reprieve, utilising his aristocratic connections in England to try to obtain this. Not satisfied with that, he wrote a violent (and anonymous) letter to the

An execution in progress at the foot of the West Bow, Edinburgh, by James Skene of Rubislaw.

London Chronicle, attacking the bias and motivation of the judge in charge of the trial, Lord Justice Clerk Miller, as 'a striking specimen of what goes on in this narrow country'. As a result, the judge's young son issued a challenge to a duel, which was only very narrowly averted (with great relief on our hero's part). That he was hot-headed, single-minded and obstinate to a fault cannot be denied. Of course, if he hadn't been so, there would have been no travels, no journals and no *Life of Johnson.*

Another illustration of Boswell's persistent wrongheadedness can be seen in his relations with his father and the latter's determination to entail the succession to the Auchinleck estate. An entail was a legal device restricting the eligible class of successors to the estate and protecting it from being burdened by debt. Lord Auchinleck's fears in this regard can perhaps be understood. In any event, the father wished to restrict the succession to Auchinleck to heirs (male or female) of his own body. Boswell wished to hold out for male succession only (out of 'old feudal principles'), even though this would have meant his own daughters being disinherited. The impasse between father and son led to much unpleasantness and, for a time, Boswell's allowance was under threat. At last, a degree of compromise was reached (males only in descent from Boswell's great-grandfather). Sir John Pringle wrote, tongue in cheek: 'I condole most sincerely with you on your getting what you had so long, so obstinately (pardon the expression) contended for, and at last obtained against your will: I mean the exclusion of your daughters from the succession to your landed property'. In the event, of course, Boswell and then his eldest son Alexander duly succeeded to the estate, and much heart-searching, on Boswell's part, could have been avoided.

Apart from the strain in his relations with his father and new stepmother, the most consistent consolation that Boswell had from his day-to-day life in this period was derived from his family. Despite his erratic behaviour, his drinking and whoring, Margaret, his wife, remained a loyal and level-headed companion. After Veronica (born March 1773), the children arrived at regular intervals: Euphemia 'Effie' (May 1774); Alexander 'Sandy' (October 1775); David (November 1776); James 'Jamie' (September 1778) and Elizabeth 'Betsy' (June 1780). Some of the most agreeable passages in the journals report on the progress of the children. Little David only survived until the next spring and there is a most affecting passage, where the grieving father lays out the little body:

> *I carried the little corpse on my arms up to the drawing room and laid it on a table covered with a table cloth, parts of which again I spread over my child. There was something of dreariness in the blank in our nursery. Yet the gentle death of the sweet innocent, and his appearance like wax work and at peace after his sufferings, affected us pleasingly... This morning Veronica and Effie would see their little brother. Veronica calmly kissed him. But Effie was violently affected, kissed him over and over again, cried bitterly, 'Oh my poor Billy, Davie', and run to his nurse, who had also been hers, and clung about her, blubbering and calling to her 'Oh come and take him off the table. Waken him, waken him and put him in his cradle.' With much difficulty we got her pacified.*

A portion of old James Court,
by James Drummond, c. 1850.

But most reports are much less poignant. Veronica is described (aged three) singing to her daddy and (aged seven) playing the harpsichord. Sandy, the Boswell heir-to-be, is given a Shetland sheltie (pony) of his own at the age of five. He is also beaten for lying that same year (as Boswell reports his father having done to him). James junior is described as a 'fine, big, strong boy' baby and as starting to speak ('here', 'here') at eighteen months. Effie is inoculated for the smallpox, as were the others, and gave cause for concern until the symptoms abated.

Boswell was concerned to inculcate the children with religious principles and family loyalty. Young Sandy was the chief object in this latter regard. All the children were taught to say prayers and psalms on a Sunday. The lessons were not always as successful as the father would have wished them to have been. On one occasion (January 1780), Boswell's description of hell and devils who would come for the children

The north frontage of James Court, to the left of the Bank of Scotland, Edinburgh, about 1812. Boswell's house on the third and fourth floors.

Old James Court on fire,
15 August 1857.

A surviving eighteenth century court (Wardrop's),
near James Court, Lawnmarket, Edinburgh.

if they were bad, was so vivid 'that they were all three suddenly seized with such terror that they cried and roared out and ran to me for protection (they and I being in the drawingroom), and alarmed their mother, who came upstairs in a fright, and she and the maid took them downstairs. This vexed me.'

There are many charming cameos, too, of the family at their summer house across the Meadows or at Drumsheugh and many pleasant family excursions to the home of Sir Alexander Dick at Prestonfield.

All this time, the family was resident in what appears to have been a double flat in James Court. Entering from that part of Edinburgh's High Street known as the Lawnmarket, the Court still forms an irregular square, flanked on all sides by high tenement buildings. Boswell's house was part of that building which formed the north-west side of the square and which looked out over the Nor' Loch and the Forth to Fife. Dr Johnson, on his 1773 visit, described it to Mrs Thrale as consisting of 'very handsome and spacious rooms; level with the ground on one side of the house, and on the other, four stories high.' The actual building was burned down in 1857 and was rebuilt as a Bank. At the time of writing, the building is now occupied (appropriately enough) by the Family Department of the Sheriff Court and the offices of the Free Church of Scotland. The ground still falls

A surviving portion of the eighteenth century north front of James Court, Edinburgh.

steeply away to the north, although the construction of the Mound has since decreased the difference between the levels to three stories. The rooms must indeed have been 'handsome and spacious', for companies of up to a dozen, including nobles and their ladies, were frequently dined by the Boswells. From the journals we know that the drawing room and dining room were upstairs and that the best bedroom (normally occupied by Boswell and his wife) was given to Dr Johnson on his visit. With two adults, five children, their nurse, sundry servants and frequent visitors, the house must have been a lively and busy place.

During this period, the Old Town was still the residence of the gentry and nobility as well as of all the other ranks. But the drift to the New Town development to the north was beginning. In 1769 Boswell defended the 'inconveniences of the old town of Edinburgh', and opined that he would never leave it. Yet, by 1782, the old family house in the Parliament Close had been sold (for a very substantial 900 guineas), and Boswell himself noted: 'I had brought my mind to remove to the New Town, as better for the health of my wife and children and to be near to my father in his new house' (in St Andrew's Square). In the meantime, the amenity of the James Court houses was maintained by a set of regulations, enforced by a committee of residents.

1. No person shall at any time throw out, from any window or door in the Court, any water, ashes, or nastiness of any kind, under the penalty of 2s 6d. for the first offence, 5s. for the second, and 10s. for the third and every other offence...

3. No person shall at any time carry a lighted candle, or other light to any one of the garrets in the Court, or cellars, under the tenement, under the penalty of 10s. 6d. for each offence, except in lanthorns...

7. That the scaffengers shall keep the forecourt, stairs and garden, free from vagrants and begging poor, of which too many frequent them without challenge...

Boswell reported (in 1776) that the residents were organising a ball, but disliking 'such corporation meetings... neither my wife nor I went to it'. Life, then, even in the Old Town of the 1770s, seems to have been comfortable enough, at least for the upper classes.

Boswell had a well-stocked legal and general library in his home. Amongst his papers survives a catalogue of his books, written by himself and dating from the early 1770s. The library includes the well-known legal textbooks of his time, some still referred to today: Lord Stair's *Institutions* (1759 ed.), Erskine's *Institutes* (1757) and, significantly perhaps, *Tracts Concerning Entails*. The extensive 'History and Miscellanies' section reflects his taste in English and European literature and the places visited on his travels. About 320 books in all are listed. So it would be in his own study that the legal papers would be dictated and the extensive correspondence and newspaper articles penned. Boswell also made much use of the Advocates Library in the Laigh Hall, beneath Parliament House, for his legal and literary studies.

From 1777 until 1783, Boswell regularly contributed a series of essays entitled 'The Hypochondriack', to the *London Magazine*. The series eventually extended to seventy in number. They covered topics as varied as money, religion, marriage, drinking and death: as varied as Boswell's own concerns, in fact. It has to be said that many of the essays now make turgid reading (a modern collected edition was published in 1951), but they do illustrate Boswell's thinking and the scope of his researches. His journals have many entries describing the author desperate for a motto or

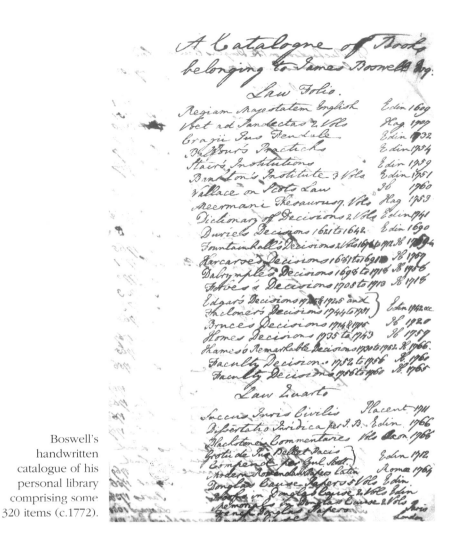

Boswell's handwritten catalogue of his personal library comprising some 320 items (c.1772).

theme and struggling to finish a number for the London post.

A publication of more direct relevance to Scotland resulted from the elevation of Robert McQueen to be a Court of Session judge, as Lord Braxfield. This is the same Braxfield who was to earn an unenviable reputation for his harshness in dealing with the radicals tried for sedition in the 1790s. Boswell's concern was at recent trends whereby the ceremony and hospitality attending on the Justiciary Courts on circuit had been curbed. There was even a suggestion that some judges had been augmenting their salaries from their circuit expenses. In a pamphlet, *Letter to Lord Braxfield,* published in May 1780 (price one shilling), Boswell anonymously upbraided His Lordship and his colleagues for any savings in either ceremony or expenses:

The old Advocates Library in the Laigh Hall, Parliament House, Edinburgh, where it remained for two and a half centuries.

The Lords of Justiciary should not contract their travelling equipage into that of a couple of private gentlemen on a jaunt of pleasure, but should remember that it is the train of a Court, composed of different members. Formerly every one of the judges had his led horse, his sumpter in the procession. The disuse of that piece of pageantry may be forgiven though not applauded. But the abolishing of a covered waggon for the baggage of the Circuit though a paltry saving, is a great grievance. Without it, how shall the mace; how shall the official clothes of the trumpeters; nay, how shall the record of Court, and the essential papers be carried? Not to mention the gowns and clothes of others who ought to be decently drest. Without it, there must be such shifts and such pinching as is to be found only in a company of strolling players. etc. etc. etc…

The trumpeters, in fact, survived into the 1960s and, it could be argued, the strolling players are still with us today! Boswell's authorship, although not publicly acknowledged, was widely suspected and another nail was driven squarely into his prospects of promotion. Boswell recorded meeting Principal Robertson in the street, when the historian commented on the *Letter:* "'It is a plain style,' said he. "But very well written," said I... "I had some scruple as to all this disguise. Yet I thought it allowable, and it was very entertaining.'"

As indicated, however, most of Boswell's writings over this period were pleadings in the many cases he conducted. One of lasting literary import secured freedom for the growing Scottish book trade from copyright restrictions contended for by their English counterparts. During the earlier years of the century there had been a continuing history of copyright prosecutions brought by English booksellers against Scottish publishers. One of those affected was Boswell's friend, Donaldson. The matter depended on the interpretation of the Copyright Act of 1710 passed in Queen Anne's time and covering both England and Scotland. On one view, the statute gave protection to the copyright holder for only fourteen years (with a further fourteen years to the author himself, if still alive). The English booksellers maintained, however, that the Act gave the owner of a copyright protection in perpetuity and there were English decisions to this effect. In the summer of 1770, Boswell found himself in court along with his friend Islay Campbell and John MacLaurin, in the defence of Alexander Donaldson and certain other booksellers. After four days of debate before a bench of thirteen judges, the great majority were for the restrictive interpretation of the Act, and Donaldson was free to publish his cheap reprints, once the statutory period of restriction had elapsed. The following year, assisted by a pamphlet penned by Boswell, Donaldson challenged the English booksellers on their own ground and appealed to the House of Lords against a contrary English decision. After much debate and much eloquence, Donaldson was again triumphant. A Jacobite clergyman noted in his diary for Saturday, 26 February 1774: 'Great rejoicings in Edinburgh upon victory over literary property; bonfires and illuminations, ordered tho' by a mob, with drum and two fifes.' Boswell told Donaldson over supper later that year that, As Alexander the Great sat down and wept that he had no more worlds to conquer, he might now, after his victory on Literary Property, sit down and weep that he had no more booksellers to conquer. We were jovial and merry.'

Boswell also frequently appeared as advocate before the General Assembly of the Church of Scotland on ecclesiastical matters. Typically, these concerned patronage (the right of a land-owner to appoint a minister to a charge) or matters of complaint by a congregation against a minister.

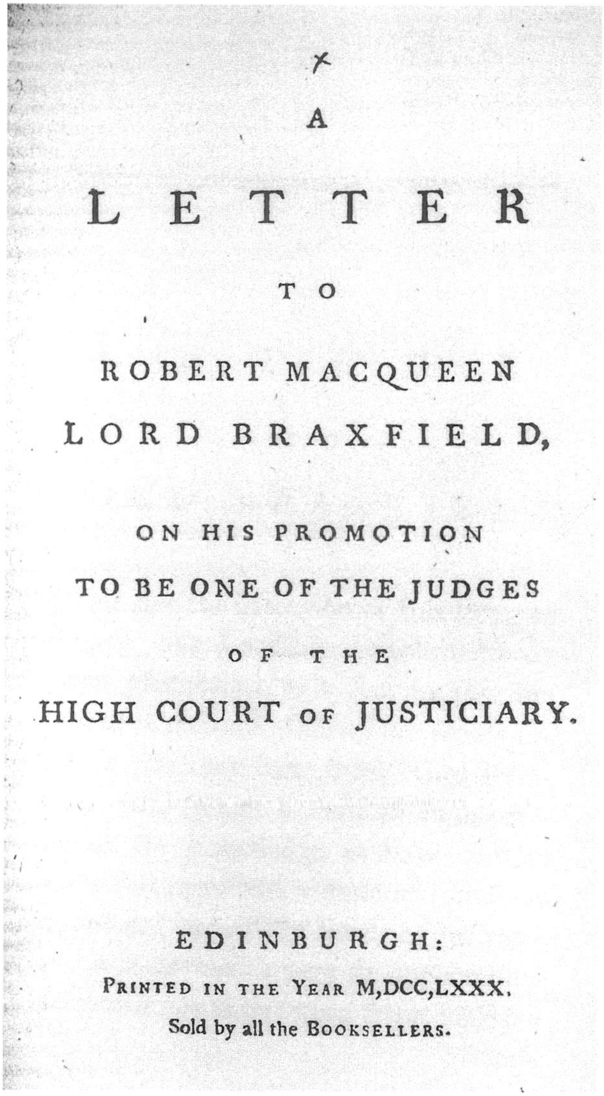

A

LETTER

TO

ROBERT MACQUEEN

LORD BRAXFIELD,

ON HIS PROMOTION

TO BE ONE OF THE JUDGES

OF THE

HIGH COURT OF JUSTICIARY.

EDINBURGH:

PRINTED IN THE YEAR M,DCC,LXXX.

Sold by all the BOOKSELLERS.

The title page of Boswell's admonitory pamphlet to the Court of Session Judges (1780).

Boswell himself thought this turgid if profitable work. His witty and irreverent colleague, John MacLaurin, saluted his efforts in verse (1770):

Sure, great was the folly
In him who Paoli
His friendship permitted to share;
To go for a guinea,
Dear Boswell, what mean ye
To plead at so humble a Bar?

Robert Macqueen,
Lord Baxfield
(1722 - 99):
successful Scottish
Advocate; hanging
judge and purported
model for Stevenson's
Weir of Hermiston
(Portrait by Raeburn).

The wicked and godly
Here jumbl'd so oddly,
For once will agree, I'm afraid,
That good honest Boswell
By no means has chose well,
Or rather mistaken his trade...

Another case, which stands out from the dozens in which Boswell appeared in the 1770s, concerned the liberty of one Joseph Knight, a negro slave. The decision was to confirm the basic abhorrence of Scots law for the status of slavery. In Boswell, Knight had an unlikely ally, because the former actually approved of certain aspects of the slave trade. Dr Johnson, on the other hand, was liberal in this regard at least, and had earlier furnished material for argument to be used in the case. Boswell himself describes it in the *Life of Johnson:*

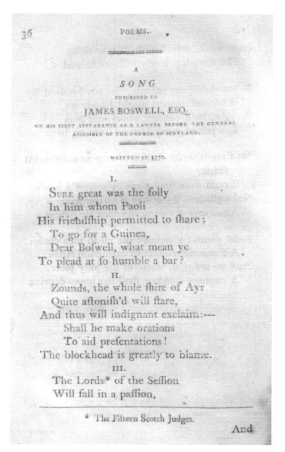

A Song by Boswell's friend, John MacLaurin, deriding his General Assembly practice.

A negro then called Joseph Knight, a native of Africa, having been brought to Jamaica in the usual course of the slave trade, and purchased by a Scotch gentleman in that Island, had attended his master to Scotland, where it was officiously suggested to him that he would be found entitled to his liberty without any limitation. He accordingly brought his action, in the course of which the advocates on both sides did themselves great honour... A great majority of the Lords of Session decided for the negro. But four of their number, the Lord President, Lord Elliock, Lord Monboddo, and Lord Covington, resolutely maintained the lawfulness of a status, which has been acknowledged in all ages and countries, and that when freedom flourished, as in old Greece and Rome.

He also takes the opportunity of slipping in a jibe at the Scottish accent of Henry Dundas, the Lord Advocate, in his generous contribution 'to the cause of the sooty stranger'.

To conclude this review of Boswell's professional affairs, it is of interest to note that he was an active Mason. In 1773 through to 1776 he was Right Worshipful Master of St John's Lodge of Canongate Kilwinning; and, in November 1776, he became Deputy Grand Master of the Freemasons in Scotland.

> *Having been applied to accept of being Deputy Grand Master of the Freemasons in Scotland, I wished to avoid it. But as worthy Sir William Forbes was to be Grand Master and thought my accepting of the office would be an obligation conferred on him, I agreed. I supped at his house this night with ten more of 'the Brethren' to concert measures. We talked with most serious importance, and I looked round the company and could not perceive the least ray of jocularity in any of their countenances. I however wondered how men could be so much in earnest about parade which is attended neither with gain nor with power; but I considered that it was really honourable to be highly distinguished in a society of very universal extent over the globe, and of which the principles are excellent. I sat till near one in the morning.*

What his friend David Hume would have made of all this can only be conjectured. Earlier in the year, Boswell had visited Hume who was then in the throes of his final illness. One of the most valuable documents left by Boswell is 'An Account of My Last Interview with David Hume Esq'. In this, he records his attempts to have the great man declare himself on the question of an after-life. Surely, at this juncture, with death nigh, he must believe in salvation?

> *He answered it was possible that a piece of coal put upon the fire would not burn; and he added that it was a most unreasonable fancy that we should exist for ever. That immortality, if it were at all, must be general; but a great proportion of the human race has hardly any intellectual qualities; that a great proportion dies in infancy before being possessed of reason; yet all these must be immortal; that a porter who gets drunk by ten o'clock with gin must be immortal; that the trash of every age must be preserved, and that new universes must be created to contain such infinite numbers. This appeared to me an unphilosophical objection, and I said 'Mr Hume, you know spirit does not take up space.'*

Two months later, at the end of August 1776, Hume was dead. Boswell and his friend, John Johnston, witnessed the burial on the Calton Hill 'concealed behind a wall till we saw the procession of carriages come down from the New Town and thereafter the procession of the corpse carried to the grave'. They then went to the Advocates Library to read some of the dead philosopher's work. Only the night before, presumably less concerned about the immortality of his soul, Boswell 'was a good deal intoxicated, ranged the streets, and having met with a comely, fresh looking girl, madly ventured to lie with her on the North Brae of the Castle Hill. I told my dear wife immediately.' Ah, Counsellor! Ah, Grand Master! Ah, Boswell!

During Boswell's middle years his ongoing relations with Auchinleck and his father continued to cause problems.

As early as April 1767, Boswell had purchased a small upland estate of Dalblair, on the eastern fringes of the Auchinleck properties. This had cost him £2,410 and was likely to bring him a rental income of about £100 a year. At first he was delighted with his status as land-owner, relished the vast prospect the estate afforded, from Ben Lomond to the Galloway hills, over Islay and Jura, and resolved to erect a pillar at the viewpoint. As the years went by, however, and the creditors were not paid, the worries of land-ownership became more apparent. Although self-avowedly a town lover, who hated the long, dreary Ayrshire nights, Boswell none the less became more committed to the estate as he grew older. During his autumn visits to Auchinleck, he would frequently ride round the policies and outlying tenancies with James Bruce, the overseer, to supervise plantings and improvements. Lord Auchinleck, however, refused to be impressed. As late as December 1779 he harshly turned down his son's offer to spend some days at Auchinleck to oversee estate affairs. 'Ye hae nae skill,' he observed. His clerk, Stobie, further aggravated the situation by suggesting that the creation of pre-existing leases would keep Boswell from 'playing the fool'.

Relations between Lord Auchinleck and his daughter-in-law were also cool. After an initial visit to Auchinleck soon after her marriage, Margaret never went again until she was mistress of the estate. Boswell was also normally at loggerheads with the second Lady Auchinleck (who he consistently refers to as the 'Noverca' (stepmother). Clearly she could have been of great use to him in gaining his father's favour; putting a word in for him, as it were. And while she occasionally did, she was normally protective of her husband and sarcastic towards his son. Swithering as to

The steading of Dalblair today, deep in the Ayrshire countryside.

whether to seek his father's permission for a trip to London in the spring of 1781, she teased him as to his lack of independence: 'A man is either a fool or physician at 40!' Added to this, Lord Auchinleck was largely indifferent to the grandchildren, apart, perhaps, from Veronica. Boswell was deeply hurt in October 1777 to realise that his father had forgotten that little David had died earlier that year.

Despite all this, Boswell remained fiercely loyal to his father and Auchinleck. As his father's powers began to fail, this sometimes showed on the bench. On one occasion, in March 1776, the judge appeared to sum up for one party but ultimately gave judgment for the other. This caused some consternation among Boswell's colleagues, Henry Dundas being notably outspoken. Boswell seriously considered a duel with the then Lord Advocate to defend his father's honour. However, a trip south cooled his ardour.

Even a man of Lord Auchinleck's constitution could not last for ever. For some years past, he had suffered acutely from a recurrent stoppage of urine, requiring catheterisation. But, in the autumn of 1782, although much failed, his spirit seemed as unyielding as ever. Two of the last exchanges noted by Boswell are not pleasant. Speaking of his brother John, who was mentally disordered, Boswell tried to persuade the old man to be sympathetic: 'He answered very harshly, "If my sons are idiots, can I help it?"' A few days later, 19 August 1782, dining at his father's house with Dr Webster, Boswell made to take a glass of claret. 'That's Dr Webster's bottle, man,' said his father with a snarl. 'If it's disagreeable to you, I shall not take any of it'... He wished to have the meanness concealed, and said, "Never fash your head." So I drank claret...'

The last act, when it came, was sudden and unexpected. Boswell and his wife had gone for a few days to Fife to visit relations. The time was a happy one. Margaret 'looked so genteel, that I was as much in love with her as a man could be'. Suddenly (29 August) a caddie on horseback arrived, with an express letter. Lord Auchinleck was dying. Boswell returned to Edinburgh at once, to find his father insensible on his deathbed. Early the next morning he notes: '... Went back. Women servants gathered. Miss Peggie: "Come and see". He was very low. Stayed in room. She carried off, Robert Boswell attending. Miss Peggie's flutter shocking. Strange thought: "Still alive, still here! Cannot he be stopped?" Breathing grew high, gradually ceased. Doctor closed eyes. Miss Peggie's exclamation. Up all night... Some time writing letters in giddy state.' At night looking at one of his father's most prized books 'from affection and nervousness, cried and sobbed'.

At first, both grief and relief were suppressed by the practical considerations of the funeral arrangements. Boswell was determined that 'all should be decent'. In fact, all was more than decent. The funeral cortege set out from Edinburgh on Monday, 2 September and journeyed via Douglas, in Lanarkshire, to Auchinleck for the funeral on the Wednesday. Boswell noted:

> *Was in agitation all the forenoon and rather awkward with the company. But... went to barn and drank health of tenants. Dinner very decent. But I was confused in mind and somewhat dreary... Felt manly all the way to church and acquiesced in the course of things. When I was carrying father to vault, was carried myself. Wandered; was in the state which I suppose a man going to execution is. Hardly was sensible of what was around me. Saw mother's coffin. Helped to deposit father. Then into our loft. Was affected much and cried.*

The expenses of the funeral were not much short of £300. If one recalls

The Boswell Mausoleum, Auchinleck Churchyard: the resting place of Lord Auchinleck and James Boswell

that the annual rental of the vast estate was about £1,500, the solemn splendour of the occasion can be envisaged.

So, at last, Boswell was Laird of Auchinleck. Dr Johnson wrote a sympathetic but counselling letter. 'You, dear sir, have now a new station, and have therefore new cares and new employments.' He advised: 'Begin your new course of life with the least show and the least expense possible; you may at pleasure increase both, but you cannot easily diminish them. Be kind to the old servants and secure the kindness of the agents and factors... From them you must learn the real state of your affairs, the character of your tenants, and the value of your lands...' Boswell replied: 'as I am very ignorant myself of country concerns and have very different opinions given me, I am perplexed how to act. I must do as well as I can at first and get more knowledge gradually. I am as sober as you would wish me to be. It was my determination that I should maintain the decorum of the representative of Auchinleck and I am doing so.' And, for the moment, at least, he was.

CHAPTER 9

The Final Years:

London and Scotland

1783-95

At first, Boswell's new status as Laird of Auchinleck did not greatly alter the pattern of his life. He continued to practise at the Scottish Bar and, for a year or two, swithered as to whether to make London his permanent base and try his luck at the English Bar.

Certainly, in his native Ayrshire, he was a man of much greater consequence now that he was the proprietor of the large Auchinleck estate. He presided over the local Quarter Sessions and organised a Loyal Address to the King from the Ayrshire Freeholders. He actively participated in the work of the Ayrshire Road Trustees. He conducted a long but ultimately unsuccessful series of negotiations to be chosen as parliamentary candidate for the county. At first he was highly pleased with his local activities. On 17 March 1784, he wrote: 'I never in my life felt myself better than I was today. I recalled to my mind all the ideas of the consequence of County meetings and of the credit of the family of Auchinleck which I had acquired from my father in my early years, and I superadded the monarchical principles which I had acquired from Dr Johnson.' The estate management was in good hands, with the loyal family overseer, James Bruce, still in charge as he had been since Boswell's childhood. When away from Auchinleck he kept in close touch and the correspondence with Bruce, and Andrew Gibb who became overseer in 1790, reveals that Boswell as laird was conscientiously involved in the management and improvement of his estate and the welfare of its tenants. The estate was augmented by the purchase of the farms of Fordmouth

The older Boswell at age 45. The now famous man of letters, painted by Sir Joshua Reynolds in 1785.

(1783), Willockshill (1785) and the little estate of Knockroon (1790).

Despite this, Boswell found that he was not rich. A significant part of his father's estate was burdened with a liferent to the Dowager Lady Auchinleck. With other charges upon, and the cost of improvements to, the estate, Boswell was left with only about £500 per year, plus his Bar earnings, to fund his new status and his growing family. As at the end of 1783, he was in overdraft to his bank to the large sum of £1,310.2s.6d. But while a number of Ayrshire land-owners (like his kinsman, John Boswell of Knockroon) were forced to sell out as a result of the collapse of the Ayr Bank in 1772, Boswell was never in any danger.

In Edinburgh, the family continued to live in James Court (rent £90 per annum). Until he finally decided to attempt the English experiment, Boswell's practice as advocate remained steady, if unspectacular. As late as February of 1785 he reports: 'My practice in the Court of Session, though not very lucrative, made a creditable appearance.' But, in truth, with the removal of paternal constraint, Boswell was becoming less and less enamoured of his practice and of Edinburgh. In November 1783, at the start of the winter term, he found: 'the vulgarity and bustle of the Court of Session . . .very disgusting after my consequence at Auchinleck.' Part of his

The *Hail Fifteen* Judges in the last sitting as a single court in July 1808.

disgust, no doubt, was that he had not been promoted to either Solicitor General or Lord Advocate, in a recent political reshuffle. Appraising himself (to himself) a few months earlier, he had concluded:

The great difficulty is to distinguish between noble ambition and foolish, restless, conceited aspiring. In my coolest moments, and after employing the powers of judgement under reflection which GOD has given me, with a fair wish to be well informed, I am clearly persuaded that a man of my family, talents and connexions may reasonably endeavour to be employed in a more elevated sphere than in Scotland, now that it is in reality only a province. But if I find after some time that there is little hope of being so employed, I shall set my mind to be satisfied with a Judge's place in Scotland.

From this generous assessment of his own worth, it can readily be concluded that Boswell was no realist. Shortly afterwards he proceeded to prove this in the most conclusive way.

In the meantime, some old friends had either departed the scene or had

Henry and Robert Dundas:
the all-powerful brothers,
as Lord President and Lord
Advocate respectively.

fallen on bad times. One of Boswell's original mentors, Lord Kames, had died at the end of December 1782. Boswell had spent quite some time with him in the weeks before. He noted in his journal for Saturday, 21 December 1782: 'Just saw him in the Court of Session like a ghost, shaking hands with Lord Kennet in the Chair, and Lords Alva and Eskgrove patting him kindly on the back, as if for the last time.' This description seems to give the lie to the apocryphal tale of Kames quitting his brethren with the salutation 'Farewell, ye bitches!' Another old friend, Andrew Crosbie, often his companion in arms in criminal cases. 'was now ruined in his circumstances and married to a strumpet'. Worse, perhaps, some of his own contemporaries were now being appointed as judges. So, how to get ahead? How to break the mould?

The way chosen by our hero was typically Boswellian. Having become reconciled to Lord President Dundas, he also tried to court his Lord Advocate son, Henry. For a time he seemed to be making progress. He then decided to throw his weight behind the Dundas-Pitt administration by publishing *A Letter to the People of Scotland* at the end of December 1783.

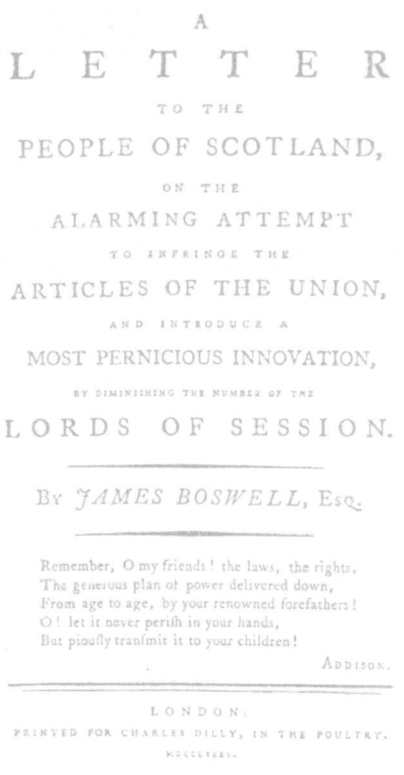

A
L E T T E R
TO THE
PEOPLE OF SCOTLAND,
ON THE
ALARMING ATTEMPT
TO INFRINGE THE
ARTICLES OF THE UNION,
AND INTRODUCE A
MOST PERNICIOUS INNOVATION,
BY DIMINISHING THE NUMBER OF THE
LORDS OF SESSION.

By *JAMES BOSWELL*, Esq.

Remember, O my friends ! the laws, the rights,
The generous plan of power delivered down,
From age to age, by your renowned forefathers !
O ! let it never perish in your hands,
But piously transmit it to your children !

ADDISON.

LONDON:
PRINTED FOR CHARLES DILLY, IN THE POULTRY.
MDCCLXXXV.

Boswell's second *Letter to the People of Scotland* (1785) which finally sunk his chances of preferment.

In this, he strongly supported the policies of the government in trying to regulate and limit the power of the East India Company. The *Letter* was quoted in a parliamentary debate by Dundas, and Pitt himself wrote to congratulate Boswell on his effort. Dundas was also reported as saying that it might have merited an office worth £200 to £300 per annum, if any had then been available. On the other hand, former friends (and potential patrons) such as Edmund Burke and Lord Mountstuart, being of the other party, were less impressed.

However, being constitutionally unable to leave well alone, Boswell shortly undid all the apparent good he had done himself. In May 1785 he composed a further *Letter*, in which he attacked the government, maligned its supporters and pilloried friend, foe and colleagues alike. The theme this time was of direct relevance to Scotland. The government proposed a Bill to diminish the number of judges of the Court of Session from the traditional fifteen to ten, while augmenting the salaries of the remainder. The proposal was probably reasonable enough (in 1830 the number was in fact diminished to thirteen at which it remained until 1948). But, of course, there were perfectly valid objections. For a start, the 'hail Fifteen' had been the complement of the court since its institution in 1532. As a traditionalist (not to mention a place-seeker), Boswell was naturally exercised by the proposal. Ten judges would be more tyrannical than fifteen. They would be more easily managed by Dundas. It was a breach of the terms of the Act of Union of 1707. What would be in danger next? The Kirk perhaps? Could swingeing new taxes be imposed? The people of Scotland were being driven like black cattle to Smithfield by Dundas, 'King Harry the Ninth'. Certainly there was no shortage of aspirants for judicial office (he mentions his own friends, MacLaurin, Nairn, and Alexander Gordon), but the proposed increase of salaries might mean that persons of base motives might wish to apply for that reason alone. He himself was writing from a pure motive as he at present had no wish for office; *he* would try *his* fortune in a wider sphere etc. And (after 100 pages or so), with a final panegyric on the virtuous ancestry of the Boswell family and a 'puff' for his forthcoming *Journal of a Tour to the Hebrides,* the *Letter* ends with his signature.

The following March, the Lord Advocate, Islay Campbell, pleasantly observed that 'he had given up the scheme of diminishing' . . . and 'said, You may be Lord of Session now, if you like it'. But alas, he did not mean it. The real power behind the appointments was Dundas, the tyrant of the *Letter.* Having abandoned his 'pure motive' Boswell petitioned Dundas in some detail (in July 1786) for a government place, pending the next available vacancy in the Court of Session. Dundas took six months to reply and then opined cruelly that Boswell's application could only be sound if his promotion would 'give satisfaction to the Bench, the Bar and Country'. In short, forget it!

By this time, Boswell had indeed resolved to try his fortune in a wider sphere. He had solicited many opinions as to his prospects at the English Bar. Some (Dr Johnson and Burke) told him that he should persevere as he was. Others were mildly encouraging. The decisive factor, however, seems to have been Boswell's increasing disenchantment with Edinburgh and its narrow, provincial sphere. Writing to Temple, in July 1784, on his return from London he stated: 'I was three nights comfortably well with my family at Auchinleck. Then my wife accompanied me to Edinburgh, where I was no sooner arrived than at once, as if plunged into a dreary vapor, my fine spirits were extinguished and I became as low and as miserable as ever. There certainly never was a mind so local as mine. How strange, how weak, how unfortunate is it that this my native city and my countrymen

Boswell, age 52,
in 1793, by George Dance.

should affect me with such wretchedness.' And to put the seal on his feelings, he had been approached by Hugh Blair, one of the Edinburgh literati, who had enquired of his eminent friend: 'Hoo did you leave Sawmuel?' So, in the spring of 1783 and 1784 Boswell was in London preparing the ground for his eventual move.

These were the last visits when he was able to spend time with Dr Johnson. The latter was now over seventy years old and in failing health. In June 1784, the two friends had visited Oxford, 'that venerable seat of learning, orthodoxy and Toryism'. Johnson had passed a year there as a student and was fiercely proud of his *alma mater*. Here was an opportunity for Boswell to gather materials as to his earlier years. Johnson also expressed a desire to visit Italy before he died and his friend made an application, via the Lord Chancellor, Thurlow, to see if some augmentation to his royal pension might be arranged to accommodate this. Unfortunately, the scheme came to nothing.

Under the date 30 June 1784, Boswell records his last parting from the great Doctor:

Sir Joshua Reynolds' coach was to set us both down. When we came to the entry of Bolt Court, he asked me if I would not go in with him. I declined it from an apprehension that my spirits would sink,. We bade adieu to each other affectionately in the carriage. When he had got down upon the foot-pavement, he called out 'Fare ye well!' and without looking back sprung away with a kind of pathetic briskness (if I may use that expression), which seemed to indicate a struggle to conceal uneasiness, and was to me a foreboding of our long, long separation.

The good doctor's health did not hold up for long and he died on 13 December that year. Receiving the dismal news in Edinburgh on the 17th, Boswell wrote: 'I was stunned, and in a kind of amaze . . . I did not shed tears. I was not tenderly affected. My feeling was just one large expanse of stupor. I knew that I should afterwards have sorer sensations.' The very next day he had a letter from his publisher, Dilly, wanting to know 'in the true spirit of the trade . . . if I could have an octavo volume of 400 pages of his conversation ready by February'. Boswell, however, was determined to do honour to his hero in a 'deliberate' fashion. And, indeed, it would be a further six and a half years before his monumental *Life* was published.

So now there were two immediate schemes: the call to the English Bar and the publication of his own *Journal* of the 1773 Tour to the Hebrides. It will be recalled that Boswell had refrained from publishing the latter during Johnson's life, although the doctor had read and approved of most of the *Journal.* Now that restraint was removed and much of 1785 was taken up in revising the account for the press. For the first time, Boswell spent the summer entirely in London and did not attend the Court of Session. The family remained in Scotland. The London stay afforded the great dual advantages of contact with his publisher and with a new literary associate, Edmond Malone, whose advice, assistance and literary skill were invaluable in the preparation of the work. After six months or so of hard labour, the *Tour* was published. On 21 September 1785, Boswell attended a Royal levée: 'The King asked me when I went North. I said "On Saturday, Sir. My book has detained me longer than I expected. But tomorrow is Coronation Day with me too. 'Finis coronat opus.' It will then be finished. Your Majesty will have it tomorrow evening."' The next night he dined at Malone's with Sir Joshua Reynolds and his friends, Langton and Dempster, 'the jury on my *Tour,* who applauded it much'. Then, leaving the literary

King George the Third,
c. 1767, in a flattering
study by Allan Ramsay.

storm to break in his absence, he headed north to his family, after an absence of six months.

The essence of the *Tour* has already been given in Chapter 7, as has an account of the furious reaction of Sir Alexander MacDonald to Boswell's strictures on his hospitality. By and large, literary London was delighted. Here was something fresh and new, with more than a whiff of scandal. Here was the great Dr Johnson 'au naturel': his every move and foible picturesquely reported by his companion. And, as for the companion . . .! The *Critical Review* of November 1785 put it thus:

> *We cannot easily leave Johnson, but his companion will not forgive us if we pass him without notice; and why should we omit to mention him, whose vivacity has confessedly enlivened the didactic gravity of the literary Colossus – whose good-humoured vanity generally pleases? Excuse us, Mr Boswell; though we sometimes smile at your volubility, yet we go with you cheerfully along. Life has too*

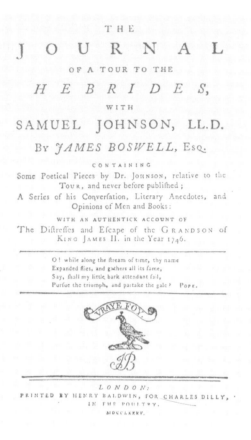

THE

JOURNAL

OF A TOUR TO THE

HEBRIDES,

WITH

SAMUEL JOHNSON, LL.D.

BY *JAMES BOSWELL,* ESQ.

CONTAINING

Some Poetical Pieces by Dr. JOHNSON, relative to the
TOUR, and never before publifhed;
A Series of his Converfation, Literary Anecdotes, and
Opinions of Men and Books:

WITH AN AUTHENTICK ACCOUNT OF

The Diftreffes and Efcape of the GRANDSON of
KING JAMES II. in the Year 1746.

O! while along the ftream of time, thy name
Expanded flies, and gathers all its fame,
Say, fhall my little bark attendant fail,
Purfue the triumph, and partake the gale? POPE.

BRAVE FOY

JB

LONDON:
PRINTED BY HENRY BALDWIN, FOR CHARLES DILLY,
IN THE POULTRY.
MDCCLXXXV.

Title page of the
Tour of the Hebrides (1785):
Boswell's version of the
famous jaunt with Dr Johnson.

many grave parts; let us catch the fluttering butterfly occasionally in
the flowery meadows; he will not detain us long and it may deceive
the length, sometimes the tediousness of the way. Mr Boswell has
drawn his own and Doctor Johnson's character: the last is delineated
with much strength and coloured with justness; the former is drawn
from the heart ...

And the *Gentleman's Magazine* of the same date opined: 'It is, with some
few exceptions, happily and vigorously written. The severity of criticism
might occasionally detect some few errors of style . . . But it would be not
only uncandid but ungrateful to dwell on a few minute blemishes after the
pleasure and profit we have received in the perusal of this work. Mr
Boswell announces a life of Doctor Johnson for which we shall wait, not
without impatience.'

Caricaturists and satirists had a field day. Rowlandson produced his
famous *Picturesque Beauties of Boswell,* including a cartoon of Boswell

'Revising for the Second Edition', under physical threat by Sir Alexander MacDonald. And one 'Peter Pindar', actually John Wolcot, successively doctor, divine and pamphleteer, published 'A Poetical and Congratulatory Epistle to James Boswell, Esq', the tone of which can be captured in the first six lines:

> *O Boswell, Bozzy, Bruce, what'er thy name,*
> *Thou mighty Shark for anecdote and fame;*
> *Thou Jackal, leading lion Johnson forth*
> *To eat McPherson midst his native North;*
> *To frighten grave professors with his roar,*
> *And shake the Hebrides from shore to shore . . .*

For once, this was not written by Boswell himself and he seems to have been quite annoyed. But he could hardly complain. First, he was being repaid in is own currency, and second, the book was a runaway success. The first impression of 1,500 copies was sold out in a little over two weeks and second and third editions were required by the end of the year. 'Corsica' Boswell had become 'Hebrides' Boswell.

At Auchinleck more mundane matters awaited. Margaret's health remained very uncertain. The children were now growing apace: Veronica was twelve, Euphemia eleven, Sandy ten, James Jr seven, and Betsy five. If Boswell was to be based in London, what was to happen to the family? As it transpired, they were to stay at James Court or Auchinleck until the whole family moved south to join him a year later (September 1786).

This time, Boswell remained in Scotland for only six weeks, when he was off south again to put arrangements in hand for his admission to the English Bar. He was called in February 1786:

> *Some time after dinner, the head porter announced a 'call'. Then I,*
> *the Hon John Eliot, and Mr William Dowdeswell, nephew of the*
> *Chancellor of the Exchequer, were introduced (with each a band,*
> *and holding a 'pileus' or black cap) into the Chamber where the*
> *benchers were sitting at table, and were told of our being called to*
> *the rank of Barristers-at-Law. I said, 'We return you 10,000 thanks*
> *for the honour that has been done us,' and then retreated. I added*
> *this ceremony to the Laird of Auchinleck, in my own consciousness.*

A few days later, the new intrants gave a grand dinner.

We were in all 16. I sat at the head of the table and Mr Dowdeswell at the foot, and a more jovial, pleasant day was never passed. I had fixed a dinner by myself. My two brethren joined me. I ordered everything. We had a course of fish, a course of ham, fowls and greens, a course of roast beef and apple pies, a dessert of cheese and fruit, Madeira port and as good claret as ever was drank. The officers of the Society attended us. And the lustre was lighted, which had not been the case for thirty years as I was told. The company dropped off gradually. Malone and Courtenay and I walked home, in excellent spirits and not drunk, towards eleven. It shall ever be in my mind 'dies memorabilis'.

Being called to the English Bar (at age forty-five) was one thing; securing any business was, of course, another. That spring he set off, full of hope, as the most junior counsel on the Circuit of the North of England Courts. Of socialising there was much, but of paying work, little or none. By the beginning of July, Boswell was already writing to Margaret: 'I am now convinced that there is no probability of my getting great practice at the English Bar… it is shocking to me, who have been used to have a competent share of practice, to be altogether without it, and I am impatient and fretful.' But (or so it seemed at least), succour was at hand.

One of the extraordinary features of the second *Letter to the People of Scotland* had been Boswell invoking the assistance of various potentates to come to the aid of the Nation. Prominent amongst these had been the name of James Lowther, First Earl of Lonsdale, and an owner of vast estates in the north of England. Having despaired of Lords Mountstuart and Douglas as patrons, Boswell was clearly angling for another. To his delight the bait was taken and he was engaged, nominally as counsel for the Mayor of Carlisle, but actually for the Lonsdale interest, in the forthcoming parliamentary elections in November and December 1786. Part of Boswell's function was to rule in favour of the voting competence of dozens of bogus freemen created by Lowther to carry his interest: 'Lowther's mushrooms', as they were known. This was the same Boswell who had been so upset when his own father had been persuaded by the Dundas faction to do much the same in relation to the Ayrshire electorate. In any event, he earned a fee of 150 guineas, his only earning of substance at the English Bar. But he also found himself in the sway of a tyrant and bully, many times more oppressive than Henry Dundas.

James Lowther,
First Earl of Lonsdale
(1736 - 1802), as a young
man: Boswell's half-mad,
tyrannical patron.

Lowther seems to have been slightly mad. He had an entourage of place-men and Members of Parliament, whom he required to go everywhere with him. Boswell would be peremptorily summonsed to accompany His Lordship to the north and then be left kicking his heels for days on end, awaiting His Lordship's pleasure. This was much to bear for a proud, if impoverished, 'old Scots Baron', and Boswell several times contemplated breaking off the relationship (once by stealing away from Lowther Castle on foot, in the snow). But Lowther could mean preferment, at least as Recorder of Carlisle (salary £20) and possibly as one of his nominee MPs. The former position was in fact secured by Boswell in January 1788 and, for a time, he revelled in his new (part-time) status as 'Mr Recorder'. The latter never was, for, after having put up with repeated humiliations and reverses, Boswell learned that Lowther had told one of his henchmen that he would never make him an MP as 'he would get drunk and make a foolish speech.' However true, *this* was too much and Boswell hastened to offer his resignation as Recorder (mid June 1790). Tyrant to the last, Lonsdale insisted that Boswell carry out his duties in Carlisle during the forthcoming election proceedings (which included a full-blown riot). A duel between patron and patronised was narrowly averted. Lonsdale: 'You will be settled when you have a bullet in your belly, Boswell (to his journal later):

> *Looking on him really as a madman, and wishing upon principle never to have a duel if I could avoid it with credit, I protested that I had no such intention as he supposed; and then in order to give him an opportunity to have the matter adjusted, I asked his pardon for using expressions which His Lordship had imagined attacked his honour, but which I solemnly declared were not so meant by me. He then said that he would not have used such words to me if he had not thought that my expressions were meant as he had supposed. Then we drank a glass of wine.*

And after a long enforced wait at Carlisle, in the depths of depression, Boswell was at last free from the 'great Lowther'.

But this is to anticipate. In September 1786, the whole family moved to London to the first of three houses which the Boswells would occupy in the city. Almost at once, there was a difference in London: with the family and its responsibilities there, the metropolis 'felt... little different from Edinburgh'. The children were placed at day schools and Margaret busied herself with making the house a home. Her health, already precarious, continued to cause grave concern. In fact, she was in the final stages of the consumption that was to take her life. Returning from a Lowther expedition in January 1788, Boswell found that Margaret had been so ill as to have been 'at the gates of death'. The only hope was to move her back to Auchinleck, and this was done in May of that year. For a time, all seemed well. In July of 1788 Boswell wrote to Malone:

> *The country air, ass's milk, the little amusements of ordering about her family, gentle exercise, and the comfort of being at home and amongst old and valuable friends has had a very benignant effect upon her; and I would fain flatter myself that she may recover, though not full health, yet such a degree of it as that she may enjoy life moderately well. Her preservation is of great importance to me and my children, so that there is no wonder that I suffer frequently from anxious apprehensions, which make me shrink. I sometimes upbraid myself for leaving her; but tenderness should yield to the active engagement of ambitious enterprise.*

The Boswell family house at 55 - 56 Great Queen Street, London,
painted in 1846 by John Archer.

By the spring of 1789, matters had become acute. Margaret had remained
at Auchinleck with Euphemia and Betsy. Boswell was in London with
Veronica, Sandy and James. On his return to Auchinleck early in April, he
found his wife 'emaciated and dejected' and 'very weak'. After a month, a
peremptory summons came from Lowther to represent his interest in the
Court of the King's Bench in London. Boswell was highly alarmed at the
thought of leaving Margaret: 'but I flattered myself she would grow better
as summer advanced, as she had done for the three former years; and both
she and I thought that there was no fear of a sudden change for the worse.
I was in great agitation and very averse to go. But she generously pressed
me to be resolute… After breakfast bid adieu tenderly, yet less in agitation
than yesterday. I never shall forget her saying, "Good journey!"' Alas, the
apprehensions proved well founded. He was hardly in London a week,
when he got news that Margaret was again seriously ill. He later wrote to
Temple:

*My two boys and I posted from London to Auchinleck night and day,
in sixty-four hours and one quarter, but alas! our haste was all in
vain. The fatal stroke had taken place before we set out. It was very
strange that we had no intelligence whatever upon the road, not*

*even in our own parish, nor till my second daughter came running
out from our house and announced to us the dismal event in a burst
of tears. O! my Temple! what distress, what tender painful regrets...*

So was his 'worthy friend' his 'dearest life' taken from him. Boswell was
never really to recover from this blow.

After Margaret's death (4 June 1789), the focus of Boswell's life turns
away from Scotland. Apart from Auchinleck, he had very largely lost
interest in things Scottish. This may explain why he appears not to have
responded to a request for an introduction made in a letter of November
1788 by Robert Burns. Burns had written '. . . I had the honor of drawing
my first breath almost in the same parish with Mr Boswell... to have been
acquainted with such a man as Mr Boswell, I would hand down to my
posterity as one of the honors of their ancestor.' Possibly, too, Boswell
would be chary of Burns's doubtful local reputation as radical and
lampooner. And Mr Boswell was, after all, 'gentry'. It is ironic to consider
that, had Burns been a Lincolnshire or Devon poet, Boswell would
probably have hastened to meet him. As it was, he noted smugly on the
letter: 'Mr Robert Burns, the Poet, expressing very high sentiments of me'.

After 1786, Boswell was only to be once more in Edinburgh, for a brief
visit in the spring of 1793. His old friends Johnston of Grange and Sir
Alexander Dick had died in the meantime. He stayed on at Auchinleck for
the summer and most of the autumn of 1789 and then was not back there
again until the end of August 1791. Estate affairs were not neglected,
however, even though old James Bruce, the faithful overseer, had died in
August 1790. A further substantial property was acquired for Auchinleck in
October 1790. This was the estate of Knockroon, which Boswell had
thought would made a suitable 'patrimony' for young James, Alexander
being heir to the rest. The acquisition cost the vast sum of £2,500, an
amount which Boswell could ill afford. Could the long-delayed publication
of the *Life* save the situation?

The preparation of the *Life of Johnson* now became the paramount
consideration. From the middle of 1786, Boswell had been busy on this,
with much help and encouragement from Malone. The arrangement of the
material itself was highly complicated. '22nd June 1786... Returned home
and sorted until I was stupified...' Anecdotes and reminiscences of Johnson
had to be coaxed from friends and acquaintances, some reluctant to entrust
such to Boswell's discretion. The 'great biographer' was frequently in near
despair. But the twin pillars of Malone and the memory of his mentor, Dr

Edmond Malone (1741 - 1812): man of letters, who encouraged and assisted Boswell in his preparation of the *Life of Johnson*.

Johnson, together, of course, with the hope of lasting fame, was enough to keep him going. At the end of November 1789 he wrote to Temple.

You cannot imagine what labour, what perplexity, what vexation I have endured in arranging a prodigious multiplicity of materials, in supplying omissions, in searching for papers buried in different masses – and all this besides the exertion of composing and polishing. Many a time have I thought of giving it up. However, though I shall be uneasily sensible of its many deficiencies, it will certainly be to the world a very valuable and peculiar volume of biography, full of literary and characteristical anecdotes... told with authenticity and in a lively manner. Would that it were in the booksellers' shops. Methinks if I had this 'magnum opus' launched, the public has no farther claim upon me.

Fanny Burney, the young novelist, then a maid-in-waiting to the Queen at Windsor, noted in her diary of October 1790 an encounter with Boswell, seeking copies of Dr Johnson's letters to her.

THE

L   I   F   E

OF

SAMUEL JOHNSON, LL.D.

COMPREHENDING

AN ACCOUNT OF HIS STUDIES
AND NUMEROUS WORKS,

IN CHRONOLOGICAL ORDER;

A SERIES OF HIS EPISTOLARY CORRESPONDENCE
AND CONVERSATIONS WITH MANY EMINENT PERSONS;

AND

VARIOUS ORIGINAL PIECES OF HIS COMPOSITION,
NEVER BEFORE PUBLISHED.

THE WHOLE EXHIBITING A VIEW OF LITERATURE AND LITERARY MEN
IN GREAT-BRITAIN, FOR NEAR HALF A CENTURY,
DURING WHICH HE FLOURISHED.

IN TWO VOLUMES.

By JAMES BOSWELL, Esq.

—————— *Quò fit ut* OMNIS
Votiva pateat veluti deſcripta tabella
VITA SENIS.—————   HORAT.

VOLUME THE FIRST.

LONDON:
PRINTED BY HENRY BALDWIN,
FOR CHARLES DILLY, IN THE POULTRY.
M DCC XCI.

Title page of the first edition
of Boswell's *Life of Johnson,*
(1791). His 'Magnum opus'.

Boswell: 'You must give me some of your choice little notes of the Doctor's; we have seen him long enough upon stilts; I want to show him in a new light. Grave Sam, and great Sam, and solemn Sam, and learned Sam – all these he has appeared over and over. Now I want to entwine a wreath of the graces across his brow; I want to show him as gay Sam, agreeable Sam, pleasant Sam; so you must help me with some of his beautiful billets to yourself.' I evaded this by declaring I had not any stores at hand. He proposed a thousand curious expedients to get at them, but I was invincible...

At last Boswell was able to write to Temple (6 April 1791):

My Life of Johnson is at last drawing to a close. I am correcting the last sheet and have only to write an advertisement, to make out a note of errata and to correct a second sheet of contents, one being done. I really hope to publish it on the twenty fifth current. My old

and most intimate friend may be sure that a copy will be sent to him.
I am at present in such bad spirits, that I have every fear concerning
it – that I may get no profit, nay, may lose – that the public may be
disappointed and think that I have done it poorly – that I may make
many enemies and even have quarrels. Yet, perhaps the very reverse
of all this may happen.

The long-awaited book was duly published on 16 May 1791 (the twenty-eighth anniversary of Boswell's first meeting with Dr Johnson). It was two volumes quarto, at two guineas – about £250 today. Despite the cost and the delay since the doctor's death, the book was a huge success. Fourteen hundred sets of the 1,750 printed were sold by the end of the year. And, in what must have been a moment of rare satisfaction for Boswell, in November the next year (1792), Dilly, the publisher, and Baldwin, the printer, settled with him for a net profit to the amount of £1,555.18s.2d. When one recalls that this sum was more than three times what Boswell could earn in a good year at the Scottish Bar, his decision to base himself in London and largely devote himself to literature makes much sense. There is little doubt, too, that the *Life* would never have appeared if Boswell had not had the encouragement of his London friends and the stimulation of the London context.

The rest of the Boswell story can be told fairly briefly. The family continued to thrive. Sandy, the heir, had been to Eton and was now studying law at Edinburgh. Young James was at Westminster School, where, despite being made drunk by the older boys and battered in a fight, he seems to have enjoyed himself. James was a sensitive, intelligent boy, his father's favourite, and a great support to him in his depressed final days. Veronica and Euphemia ('Phemie') were a constant trial to their father. They remained adamantly Scottish, despite Boswell's attempts to anglicise them. Temple's daughter, Nancy, described them as: 'boisterous and unpleasant' and Veronica as 'really vulgar' and speaking 'broad Scotch'. Betsy, on the other hand, pleased her father with her English accent, although she had to scold him for having been 'too fond' towards a fourteen-year-old school mate. Boswell: '... Let me be on my guard, first, against intoxication, and, secondly, at least against its improper effects...'

After the *Life* there was little for Boswell to do. He prepared for a second edition – also a success. He interested himself in the case of some convicts who had escaped from Botany Bay, and survived a horrific journey in an open boat across the Timor Sea. He dined with such of his old friends as were left. He consistently drank too much in an effort to offset depression. In June 1793 he was robbed and badly injured while returning home drunk. In October of that year, a friend noted in his diary that Boswell was 'much altered for the worse in appearance'. Clearly, he missed Margaret very much and could not seriously consider another wife. In December 1794, he wrote:

> *'Tis o'er, 'tis o'er, the dream is o'er*
> *And Life's delusion is no more*

There is, however, a last cheerful picture of the family at Auchinleck during the summer and autumn of 1794. The girls, having got over their 'wild nonsense about London', settled into country and county life. Sandy had meantime acquired a 'loud familiarity of manners', together with a very broad pronunciation, and was off to the Leith races. He could not wait for the shooting season to begin. Parties were given for the young people. There was generally more life about the place than for some years. On Christmas Day 1794 Boswell wrote to young Jamie that he had: 'sat down by myself in my own dining room to excellent leek soup, a roast turkey and a minced pie, with all which, having regaled myself sufficiently, I drank a bottle of rich gold wine. In the evening I had coffee and Edinburgh seed-cake, but I read devoutly the service for the day, morning and evening.'

The final months of Boswell's life were spent back in London at the family home at 47 Great Portland Street. He continued to interest himself in public and literary affairs. He continued to drink to excess. Then, suddenly, during a meeting of the Club ('much changed since Doctor Johnson's day') on 14 April 1795 Boswell was taken very ill and had to be carried home. In the succeeding weeks he rallied, but, by 8 May, he was so weak that young James had to complete a letter to Temple for him.

> *Alas! my friend, what a state is this. My son James has to write for me what remains of this letter and I am to dictate. The pain, which continued for so many weeks, was very severe indeed, and when it went off, I felt myself quite well, but I soon felt a conviction that I was by no means as I should be, being so excessively weak as my miserable attempt to write to you afforded a full proof. All, then, that can be said is that I must wait with patience.*

On the 19th, Boswell's brother, David, wrote:

The finely carved Boswell family crest on the wall of the family mausoleum, Auchinleck Churchyard.

> *I have now the painful task of informing you that my dear brother expired this morning at two o'clock. We have both lost a kind, affectionate friend, and I shall never have such another. He has suffered a great deal during his illness, which has lasted five weeks, but not much in his last moments; may God Almighty have mercy upon his soul and receive him into His Heavenly Kingdom. He is to be buried at Auchinleck, for which place his sons will set out in two or three days; they and his two eldest daughters have behaved in the most affectionate, exemplary manner during his confinement.*

Boswell was only fifty-four at the time of his death.

The funeral ceremony took place at Auchinleck on 8 June 1795, with Sandy and Jamie in attendance. The body was interred there in the family vault, where it still lies: its 'long home', as Boswell himself had described it. Mounted on the wall outside is a handsome carving of the family crest of the hooded hawk and the Boswell motto: 'Vraye Foy'. And, whatever else may be said about James Boswell, he did keep faith with family and friends. He also kept faith with himself and his homeland. He had the faith to persevere with the greatest biography of his time. He persevered in recording one of the most self-revealing and valuable journals ever written. And, whatever his feelings latterly about Scotland, he lies buried, not in London, but in the heart of Ayrshire.

CHAPTER 10

Boswell and Scotland:

The Legacy

In the immediate aftermath of Boswell's death, his friends and family missed him sorely. Within a week of his death, Malone wrote: 'I shall miss him more and more every day... Poor fellow, he has somehow stolen away from us without notice... Sir William Forbes, his banker and executor, wrote to Veronica describing him as 'a friend, with whom I had lived in the strictest intimacy for thirty six years, and to whose steady and unalterable regard and attachment, I shall ever look back with gratitude and affection'. Temple, his oldest surviving companion and correspondent, visited the Boswell home in London about six weeks after his death and was 'much affected on entering Mr B's house'. Boswell, then, was a man of great vivacity with a happy knack of entertaining people and putting them at ease. Another friend, years after the event, wrote that his 'place is never to be supplied.'

The public, too, were generous to the author who had given them the works on *Corsica,* the *Hebrides* and the *Life of Doctor Johnson.* The *Gentleman's Magazine* of June 1795 published tributes to his memory by his friends Malone and Courtenay. In the 1801 Supplement to the Third Edition of the *Encyclopaedia Britannica,* almost two pages were devoted to his biography and his *Life* is described as 'the most finished picture of an eminent man that ever was executed'. *Lemprier's Biographical Dictionary* of 1808 described him as having 'a warm, open and generous heart'. And the *Life,* that self-erected memorial to his hero Dr Johnson (and to himself), had, by the late 1820s, gone through at least ten official editions.

Inevitably, there was a reaction against his reputation. It had its origins in a literary feud between two of the most eminent critics of the 1830s. In 1831, a completely new edition of the *Life* was published by John Wilson Croker. This work considerably expanded upon earlier editions and was scholarly and valuable, if diffuse. But Croker had a formidable enemy in Thomas Babington Macaulay, that bombastic creator of many a purple passage. Croker and Macaulay were rival politicians as well as rival reviewers in the heady years leading up to the 1832 Reform Bill. Macaulay seized his chance and savaged Croker's new edition in a devastating article in the *Edinburgh Review* of September 1831. Not satisfied with abusing Croker, Macaulay then turned his vitriolic pen on Boswell himself. The thrust of this part of his essay was 'How could such a worthless fool write such an immortal biography?' According to Macaulay, Boswell was utterly wanting in 'logic, eloquence, wit, taste... all those things generally considered as making a book valuable... He had, indeed, a quick observation and a retentive memory. These qualities, if he had been a man of sense and virtue, would scarcely of themselves have sufficed to make him conspicuous; but, as he was a dunce, a parasite, and a cockscomb they had made him immortal.' In fact, this was all well-expressed nonsense.

Boswell's personal cause was not helped either by another massive review of the same edition, this time by the doughty Thomas Carlyle. By his account, Boswell was a 'wine bibber, and gross liver'. He was 'vain, heedless, a babbler...' The underpart of his face was 'of a low, almost brutish character'. According to the Ecclefechan Sage, Boswell's 'grand intellectual talent', was an 'unconscious' one. Once more, it was amazing that such a man could have produced such a work.

Not only did these reviews create a literary sensation, much of the mud gratuitously thrown at Boswell stuck to his reputation. By now, we are in the age of Victorian morality and the 'reprehensible passages', either gaily admitted or heavily hinted at by Boswell, were quite enough to confirm his reputation as a fool and a sot in the public eye. Most literary men knew otherwise, of course, but thus Boswell remained in the mind of the general reader. As late as 1891, the author of *Literary Landmarks of Edinburgh* saw fit to describe him as a 'silly little Scottish Laird', albeit the author of a biography 'which is the best in any language and the model for all others'.

The rehabilitation of Boswell's reputation was some time in being achieved. The first detailed study of Boswell and his family appeared in a 200-page Memoir, written in 1874 by the Rev Charles Rogers, a prolific writer on matters Scottish in the late nineteenth century. He concluded that Macaulay's assertion that the *Life* 'was due to the author's weakness, requires no serious refutation'. In fact, Boswell was the best fitted for the task. His 'perceptive power was of the highest order...' He had 'produced the best biography in the language'. In 1891 Percy Fitzgerald published a two-volume biography in which he tried to balance the savage earlier criticism against the undeniable achievement. And, five years later, W. K. Leask produced a short biography in the Famous Scots Series, which concluded (again in a rather self-contradictory way) that, although Boswell was not, perhaps, 'in any final sense, a great writer... he has created in literature and biography a revolution, and produced a work whose surpassing merits and value are known the more that it is studied.'

The tide against Boswell's reputation was then set to turn. In 1887 George Birkbeck Hill published his new six-volume edition of the *Life* Described by Professor Pottle (in his *Literary Career of James Boswell Esq*) as having so long 'held the field as the one edition for scholarly use that it is most unlikely it will ever be superseded', the work was compiled after a radically different system from previous editions. Much Boswellian material was added and the unique contribution of the original author was put into proper perspective. Hill wrote that the reader of the *Life* 'will rapidly pass through one of the most charming narratives that the world has ever seen, and if his taste is uncorrupted by modern extravagancies, will recognise the genius of an author who, in addition to other great qualities, has an admirable eye for the just proportions of an extensive work, and who is the master of a style that is as easy as it is inimitable'. Hill also produced, in 1890, his charming *Footsteps of Doctor Johnson* (mentioned in Chapter 7), in which he retraced the steps of his two heroes on their way to the Western Isles, and effectively rekindled interest in the *Journal of a Tour to the Hebrides*. He also devotes several pages to Boswell's own merit and discreetly deplores the fact that these merits appeared then to be so hidden to Boswell's descendants.

What happened to the immediate descendants? Poor Veronica's history is shortly told. Succumbing to the family curse of consumption, she survived her father by only four months, dying, aged twenty-two, on 26 September 1795. No doubt the trauma of her father's death had hastened her own end. Euphemia appears to have become quite eccentric. She attempted to support herself by miscellaneous and musical writings. She petitioned for support all connected in any way with her family. Apart from her own meagre allowance, she was in fact given a government pension of £50 per annum, presumably as a distressed relation of the great biographer. Her condition became acute and she had to be confined in a

Sir Alexander (Sandy) Boswell
(1775 - 1822), Boswell's
brilliant, irascible son,
killed in a duel, aged 46.

private asylum. Her will is none the less said to have been lucidly written,
although she requested to be buried in St Paul's Cathedral, as near as
possible to Dr Johnson (who was in fact buried in Westminster Abbey).
She died in 1837, aged sixty-three. Betsy fell in love with her cousin,
William Boswell, and married him, against her brother Alexander's wishes.
Her husband became Sheriff of Berwickshire and there were four children.
She died in 1814. James junior fulfilled his father's expectations by
becoming a studious, literary-minded man. He retained his father's
connection with Malone (who died in 1812) and assisted him in the
production of the posthumous twenty-one-volume edition of
Shakespeare's works, which eventually appeared in 1821. He became an
English barrister, and, latterly, a Commissioner for Bankruptcy. He died,
unmarried, aged forty-three, in February 1822.

Alexander, the Boswell heir, has been kept to last, as his story is by far
the most extraordinary. He was the child who apparently most fully
inherited Boswell's personality. He was a high Tory, enormously proud of
Auchinleck. He was a bibliophile and established a private printing press
at the family home. He became a fine, and quite famous poet in the Scots
vernacular, and was instrumental in having the Burns Monument erected

at Alloway. He was much more successful in achieving political advancement than his father had been. He was a Member of Parliament for an English constituency. He was made the first (real) Baron of Auchinleck in 1821 in recognition of his services as colonel commanding the Ayrshire Yeomanry Cavalry and helping to crush the Radical Rising of 1820. He was a great friend of Sir Walter Scott. Most significant of all, he inherited his father's delight in lampooning others in print, particularly on the political front. This last trait was to prove his undoing.

In the course of 1821, a series of vicious attacks on the local Whig faction had appeared in the Tory press in Edinburgh and Glasgow. In particular, personal jibes had been directed at a leading Whig land-owner, James Stuart of Dunearn, in Fife. For example, when it was proposed that Caroline, the disgraced Queen of George IV, might have been asked to visit Scotland, the *Beacon* newspaper did not think 'that anyone above the rank of Mr James Stuart would desire to be presented to her'. Stuart, understandably, was furious. He attacked and beat the editor of the paper in the street. It was then rumoured that he had declined to fight a duel with the man concerned. Taking up the campaign, the Glasgow *Sentinel* published a series of allegations of cowardice and worse against him. Stuart sued for damages and forced a co-proprietor of the *Sentinel* to reveal the identity of the virulent contributor. And who should he turn out to be but a person with whom Stuart had hitherto thought himself to be on good terms, Alexander Boswell of Auchinleck. Stuart, smarting under the earlier accusations of cowardice, issued a challenge to a duel. Alexander, being made of sterner and rasher stuff than his father, accepted. On 22 March 1822, just a month after the death of James junior, the two antagonists faced one another, armed with pistols, in a field near Auchtertool in Fife. Boswell fired in the air. Stuart did not, and Boswell was mortally wounded. Stuart fled to France but returned to face a trial for murder. He was defended by those formidable Whig lawyers Jeffrey and Cockburn. After a spirited defence in which the whole sorry affair was rehearsed, the jury acquitted him. Stuart went to America for two years and wrote a very readable book about his travels. Alexander Boswell was buried at Auchinleck. He is recalled by Cockburn in his *Memorials* as being overbearing, boisterous and addicted to coarse personal ridicule: 'His natural place was at the head of a jovial board when everyone laughed at his exhaustless spirits but each trembled lest he should be the object of the next story or song.' With Alexander's death, the last direct echo of James Boswell seems to have died.

Looking down Lady Stair's Close
from the Lawnmarket to the
Writer's Museum, only yards
from Boswell's Edinburgh home.

But the twentieth century was to see a great resurgence of interest in the biographer. For 100 years or so after Boswell's death, it was thought that his personal papers had been destroyed. Generally, the family was not sympathetic to enquiries about any document that might remain. One early biographer (Fitzgerald) even opined: 'It may be questioned if there was anything really worth preserving. A book, founded on such materials by Boswell himself, would have been welcome, but in other hands would have had little value.' Nothing, of course, could be further from the truth.

The whole fascinating story of the discovery of the Boswell papers is recounted, most readably, by David Buchanan in *The Treasure of Auchinleck* and in Professor Pottle's *Pride and Negligence*.

At first, just scraps or isolated items appeared. Letters to Temple were found in a French fishmonger's shop in about 1840, being used as wrapping paper. The 'Boswelliana' edited by Rogers had apparently escaped family destruction by having been in the library of James junior at the time of his death. Could there be more?

In the early years of this century, American scholars became interested. In 1922 Professor Chauncey B. Tinker of Yale produced his admirable *Young Boswell,* stimulating, once more, public interest in the man. It was then learned that there was in fact a considerable quantity of papers at Malahide Castle, near Dublin, the home of Boswell's great-granddaughter, Lady Talbot. In a series of delicate and expensive negotiations, the American collector Ralph Isham managed to secure the manuscripts that then came to light. They were published in an eighteen-volume limited edition between 1928 and 1934. Further papers were then discovered at Malahide in a croquet box, including the bulk of the manuscript of the Tour to the Hebrides. No sooner had Isham managed to acquire the new discoveries than a further vast batch of papers was discovered at Fettercairn House, near Aberdeen, by Professor Abbot of the university there. These had formed part of papers accumulated by Boswell's friend and executor, Sir William Forbes. After a long-drawn-out litigation in the Scottish courts, these and other papers were eventually secured by Isham and passed by him to Yale University, which had secured funding for their purchase. And it is at Yale, in the impressive modern Beinecke Rare Books Library, that the bulk of the Boswell papers are now stored. Since 1950 volumes of the *Journals* have been appearing under the Yale auspices. This series has recently (1989) been completed with the publication of the fourteenth volume, covering the final years to Boswell's death. In the meantime, two definitive volumes of biography, by Frederick Pottle and Frank Brady, covering the earlier and later years of Boswell's life, have also been published. In the international context, due honour has been done to James Boswell.

But has it truly been so done in his native land? From the Scottish viewpoint, it is regrettable that it has been American scholarship and funding that has largely secured the material for posterity. Would there ever have been sufficient Scottish awareness and effort to build anything like the impressive literary monument that Yale has erected to Boswell? Has it perhaps taken the Transatlantic perspective truly to appreciate the greatness of the man? Does Scotland, even yet, realise that it has a fourth literary great to add to its cherished triumvirate of Burns, Scott and Stevenson? There is promise in that Edinburgh University Press has recently become partner with Yale in publication of the Research Edition of Boswell's Private Papers, which will require more than thirty volumes to complete. Apart from this, there is only a small plaque at the entry to James Court recording the fact of Boswell having lived and entertained Dr

Johnson there. But is it not truly ironic that, scarcely fifty yards from the site of Boswell's home for more than a dozen years, the Writers Museum in Lady Stair's House presently makes no mention whatsoever of one of the greatest authors in the English language. Tragic also, is it not, that Auchinleck House, the scene of so much of Boswell's creative work, presently stands bleak and empty, apparently without a suitable use. Could it not, should it not, be publicised, worldwide, as a shrine to a literary great?

Perhaps now, 200 years from Boswell's death, old Edinburgh and obdurate Scotland can forgive the errant son his 'reprehensible passages' and his latter-day sneering at Scots provincialism? Boswell is recognised almost everywhere else as a literary figure of great standing. It is time he was recognised as such in his native land.

Bibliography

I ORIGINAL WORKS

Account of Corsica, 1768. The journal of the tour of the island reprinted in *Boswell on the Grand Tour: Italy, Corsica and France* (see under Journals below).

Journal of a Tour to the Hebrides with Samuel Johnson LL.D., 1785. Many subsequent editions (see under Journals below).

The Life of Samuel Johnson LL.D., 1791. Many subsequent editions. Scholarly edition edited by G. Birbeck Hill, revised by L.F. Powell, 6 Vols, Oxford, 1934 – 40.

Boswell's Column, edited by Margery Bailey, Wm Kimber, 1951. His 70 contributions to the *London Magazine,* as 'The Hypochondriac'.

II JOURNALS

Journal of the Harvest Jaunt, (autumn 1762), 1951. Available only in the deluxe edition of the *London Journal* (see below).

Boswell's London Journal (1762 – 63), edited by Frederick A. Pottle, McGraw-Hill/Heinemann, 1950.
Boswell in Holland (1763 – 64), edited by Frederick A. Pottle, McGraw-Hill/Heinemann, 1952.

Boswell on the Grand Tour: Germany and Switzerland (1764), edited by Frederick A. Pottle, McGraw-Hill/Heinemann, 1953.

Boswell on the Grand Tour: Italy, Corsica and France (1765 – 66), edited by Frank Brady and Frederick A. Pottle, McGraw-Hill/Heinemann, 1955

Boswell: In Search of a Wife (1766 – 69), edited by Frank Brady and Frederick A. Pottle, McGraw-Hill/Heinemann, 1957.

Boswell for the Defence (1769 – 74), edited by William K. Wimsatt Jr. and Frederick A. Pottle, McGraw-Hill/Heinemann, 1960.

Boswell's Journal of a Tour to the Hebrides with Samuel Johnson 1773, edited by Frederick A. Pottle and Charles H., Bennett, McGraw-Hill/Heinemann, 1963.

Boswell: The Ominous Years (1774 – 76), edited by Charles Ryskamp and Frederick A. Pottle, McGraw-Hill/Heinemann, 1963.

Boswell: In Extremes (1776 – 78), edited by Charles McC Weis and Frederick A. Pottle, McGraw-Hill, 1970.

Boswell: Laird of Auchinleck (1778 – 82), edited by Joseph W. Reed and Frederick A. Pottle, McGraw-Hill, 1977. Reprinted, Edinburgh University Press, 1993.

Boswell: The Applause of the Jury (1782 – 85), edited by Irma S. Lustig and Frederick A. Pottle, McGraw-Hill/Heinemann, 1981.

Boswell: The English Experiment (1785 – 89), edited by Irma S. Lustig and Frederick A. Pottle, McGraw-Hill, 1986.

Boswell: The Great Biographer (1789 – 95), edited by Marlies K. Danziger and Frank Brady, McGraw-Hill, 1989.
The Journals of James Boswell, 1761 – 95, selected and introduced by John Wain, Heinemann, 1991.

III CORRESPONDENCE

Letters of James Boswell to the Rev. W.J. Temple, edited by Thos. Seacombe, 1908. This will shortly be superseded by a comprehensive edition in two volumes being edited by Thomas Crawford.

Letters of James Boswell, edited by C.B. Tinker, 2 vols, Oxford University Press, 1924

Yale Research Edition Correspondence:
   Vol. I, *With John Johnston of Grange,* edited by Ralph S. Walker, McGraw-Hill/Heinemann, 1966.
   Vol. II *Relating to the Making of the Life of Johnson,* edited by Marshall Waingrow, McGraw-Hill/Heinemann, 1970.
   Vol. III, *Correspondence with Certain Members of the Club,* edited by C.N. Fifer, McGraw-Hill/Heinemann, 1976.
   Vol. IV, *Correspondence with Garrick, Burke and Malone,* edited by Peter S. Baker *et al.,* McGraw-Hill/Heinemann, 1986.
   Vol. V, *General Correspondence 1766 – 1769 (Vol 1 1766 – 67),* edited by Richard C. Cole *et al.,* Yale/Edinburgh University Press, 1993.

IV   BOSWELL PAPERS

Buchanan, David, *The Treasure of Auchinleck,* McGraw-Hill, 1974.

Pottle, Frederick A., *Pride and Negligence,* McGraw-Hill, 1982.

Pottle, Marion S. *et al., Catalogue of the Boswell Papers Held at Yale University,* 3 vols, Yale/Edinburgh University Press, 1993.

V   BIBLIOGRAPHY

Browne, Anthony E., *Boswellian Studies,* Archon Books, 1972.
Pottle, Frederick A., *The Literary Career of James Boswell Esq,* Oxford University Press, 1929. Reprinted 1966.

VI   BIOGRAPHY

EARLY WORKS (PRIOR TO DISCOVERY OF BOSWELL PAPERS)

Fitzgerald, Percy, *Life of James Boswell,* 2 vols, Chatto and Windus, 1891.

Leask, W. K., *James Boswell,* Famous Scots Series, 1896.

Rogers, Charles, *James Boswell,* London, for the Grampian Club, 1874.

Tinker, C.B., Young Boswell, Putnam, 1922.

LATER WORKS

Brady, Frank, *Boswell's Political Career,* Yale University Press, 1965.

Brady, Frank, *James Boswell, The Later Years 1769–1795,* McGraw-Hill/Heinemann, 1984.

Pottle, Frederick A., *James Boswell, The Earlier Years 1740–1769,* McGraw–Hill/Heinemann, 1966.

OTHERS

Daiches, David, *James Boswell and His World,* Thames and Hudson, 1976.

Finlayson, Iain, *The Moth and the Candle,* Constable, 1984.
Pearson, Hesketh, *Johnson and Boswell,* Heinemann, 1958.

Vulliamy, C.E., *James Boswell,* Geoffrey Bles, 1932.

Windham-Lewis, *The Hooded Hawk*, Eyre and Spottiswoode, 1946.

VII ASSOCIATED TOPICS

FOOTSTEPS

Delaney, Frank, *A Walk to the Western Isles After Boswell and Johnson*, Harper Collins, 1993.
Hill, G. Birkbeck, *Footsteps of Dr Johnson*, 1890. Reprinted in facsimile by Scolar Press, *c.*1980.

McLaren, Moray, *Corsica Boswell*, Secker and Warburg, 1966.

McLaren, Moray, *The Highland Jaunt*, Jarrolds, 1954.

Shenker, Israel, *In the Footsteps of Johnson and Boswell*, Houghton Mifflin, 1982.

BOSWELL CIRCLE

Bettany, Lewis (ed), *Diaries of William Johnston Temple*, Oxford, 1929.

Hilles, Frederick W. (ed), *Portraits by Sir Joshua Reynolds*, McGraw-Hill/Heinemann, 1952.

Hyde, Mary, *The Impossible Friendship: Boswell and Mrs Thrale*, Chatto and Windus, 1973.

BACKGROUND

Crawford, Thomas, *Boswell, Burns and the French Revolution*, Saltire Society, 1990.

Kay's Original Portraits, 2 vols, A & C Black, 1877.

Ramsay, John, of Ochtertyre, *Scotland and Scotsmen in the 18th Century*, 2 vols, Blackwood and Sons, 1888.

Stewart, Francis, *The Douglas Cause*, Notable Scottish Trials Series, Hodge and Company, 1909.

Turberville, A.S. (ed), *Johnson's England*, 2 vols, Oxford, 1933. Reprinted.

Index

HMSO publications are available from:

HMSO Publications Centre
(Mail, fax and telephone orders only)
PO Box 276, London, SW8 5DT
Telephone orders 071-873-9090
General enquiries 071-873-0011
(queuing system in operation for both numbers)
Fax orders 071-873 8200

HMSO Bookshops
71 Lothian Road, Edinburgh, EH3 9AZ
031-228 4181 Fax 031-229 2734
49 High Holborn, London, WC1V 6HB
071-873 0011 Fax 071-873 8200 (counter service only)
258 Broad Street, Birmingham, B1 2HE
021-643 3740 Fax 021-643 6510
33 Wine Street, Bristol, BS1 2BQ
0272 264306 Fax 0272 294515
9-21 Princess Street, Manchester, M60 8AS
061-834 7201 Fax 061-833 0634
16 Arthur Street, Belfast, BT1 4GD
0232 238451 Fax 0232 235401

HMSO's Accredited Agents
(see Yellow Pages)

and through good booksellers

Printed in Scotland for HMSO by CCNo 13129 35C 10/94